The Social Mind

D1521284

SERIES IN LANGUAGE AND IDEOLOGY

Edited by Donaldo Macedo

Literacy and Empowerment: The Meaning Makers
Patrick L. Courts

The Social Mind: Language, Ideology, and Social Practice
James Paul Gee

The Social Mind

Language, Ideology, and Social Practice

James Paul Gee

SERIES IN LANGUAGE AND IDEOLOGY

EDITED BY

Donaldo Macedo

BERGIN & GARVEY

New York • Westport, Connecticut • London

Copyright Acknowledgments

The author and publisher gratefully acknowledge permission to reprint extracts from the following:

James Paul Gee, *Literacy, Discourse, and Linguistics: Essays by James Paul Gee.* Special issue of the *Journal of Education*, 171 (1989), edited by Candace Mitchell.

Sarah Michaels, "Literacy as Reasoning within Multiple Discourses: Implications for Policy and Educational Reform." Paper presented to the Council of Chief State School Officers Summer Institute on Restructuring Learning. Reprinted by permission of the author.

Amy Shuman, *Storytelling Rights: The Use of Oral and Written Texts by Urban Adolescents* (Cambridge, England: Cambridge University Press, 1986).

Library of Congress Cataloging-in-Publication Data

Gee, James Paul.
    The social mind : language, ideology, and social practice / James
Paul Gee.
       p.   cm.—(Language and ideology series)
    Includes bibliographical references and index.
    ISBN 0-89789-248-8 (alk. paper).—ISBN 0-89789-249-6 (pbk. :
alk. paper)
    1. Sociolinguistics. 2. Social psychology. I. Title.
II. Series.
P40.G45   1992
306.4'4—dc20   91-36812

British Library Cataloguing in Publication Data is available.

Library of Congress Catalog Card Number: 91-36812
ISBN: 0-89789-248-8 (hb.)
     0-89789-249-6 (pb.)

First published in 1992

Bergin & Garvey, One Madison Avenue, New York, NY 10010
An imprint of Greenwood Publishing Group, Inc.

Printed in the United States of America

The paper used in this book complies with the
Permanent Paper Standard issued by the National
Information Standards Organization (Z39.48-1984).

10 9 8 7 6 5 4 3 2 1

CONTENTS

FOREWORD

Paraphrasing Paulo Freire, Jim Gee's book *The Social Mind* should have been published many years ago not only because it denudes the ideology that creates and sustains false dichotomies rigidly delineated by disciplinary boundaries but also because it represents a courageous challenge to the ideology that informs the view that "hard science," "objectivity," and "scientific rigor" must be divorced from the messy data of "soft science" and the social and political practices that generate these categories in the first place. In other words, those linguists and psycholinguists who "believe that what they study has little to do with social values or politics in any sense" fail to realize that their research results are "the product of a particular model of social structure that gear the theoretical concepts to the pragmatics of the society that devised the . . . model to begin with."[1] That is, if the results are presented as facts determined by a particular ideological framework, "these facts cannot in themselves get us beyond that framework."[2] Too often the positivistic overemphasis on hard science and "absolute objectivity" has given rise to a form of "scientism" rather than science and "specialism" rather than specialization. Intellectualists of this sort have often contributed to a further fragmentation of knowledge due to their reductionistic view of the act of knowing. They have repeatedly ignored that their very claim of objectivity is, in fact, an ideological act. Objectivity always contains within it a dimension of subjectivity; thus it is dialectical.

The importance of Jim Gee's book *The Social Mind* goes beyond his adoption of the Connectionism Theory of the mind/brain which argues that "there are no memories, meanings, or beliefs without social practices, and the social practices do not reside in anyone's head." Its significance also depends on Frei Betto's conceptualization of clarity of reality, which requires that a person transcend "the perception of life as a pure biological process to arrive at a perception of life as a biographical, and collective process."[3] Frei Betto views his concept as "a clothesline of information." In other words, "On the clothesline we may have a flux of information and yet remain unable to link one piece of information with another. A politicized person is one who can sort out the different and often fragmented pieces contained in the flux."[4] The apprehension of clarity of reality requires a high level of political clarity, which can be achieved by sifting through the flux of information and relating each piece so as to gain a global comprehension of the facts and their raison d'être. In what follows, I want to use the Gulf War as an example of how questions of language and ideology can be used to separate events from their historical contexts so as to remap a self-serving history that feeds the recontextualization of a distorted and often false reality.

It is then not a coincidence that during the Gulf War we were saturated with information around the clock in the comfort of our homes and yet we remained poorly informed. It is also not a coincidence that George Bush categorically and arrogantly stated there will be "no linkage" in any possible diplomatic settlements in the Gulf crisis. Besides the necessary linkages to create conditions for a diplomatic solution to the Gulf crisis, Bush's insistence on "no linkage" served to eclipse historicity so as to further add to a total social amnesia. How else could we explain that a highly developed society that prides itself on its freedom of information and high democratic values could ignore the clarity of the obvious? I say the clarity of the obvious because it is well known that the Reagan-Bush decade was characterized by a total disdain for the United Nations. The Reagan-Bush administration stopped paying the U.S. membership contribution to the United Nations and threatened to withdraw from the world body because the rest of the world was not subservient enough to U.S. interests. And yet, during the Gulf crisis, the same George Bush saw it convenient to hail the United Nations as the theater where "civilized" nations uphold international laws and high principles. If it had not been for the denial of linkage and the social amnesia, we could have easily have referred to Daniel Patrick Moynihan's role as ambassador to the United Nations. In his memoirs, *A Dangerous Place,* Moynihan discusses the invasion of East Timor by Indonesia and sheds light on his role as the U.S. ambassador to the United Nations: "The U.S. government wanted the United Nations to be rendered ineffec tive in any measures that it undertook. I was given the responsibility and I filled it with no inconsiderable success. "[5] Moynihan later proudly recounts his success when he states that "within two months, reports indicated that Indonesia had killed about 60,000 people. That is roughly the proportion of the population that the Nazis had killed in Eastern Europe through World War II. "[6] By not linking these historical events, the Bush administration was able to exalt a moral high ground in the defense of international laws and the sanctity of national borders during the Gulf crisis.

The U.S. defense of high principles and international laws that led to the Gulf War could only have moral currency if we were to obliterate our memory of recent history. Before proceeding, let me make it very clear that Saddam Hussein's invasion of Kuwait was brutal, cruel, and unforgivable. But the violation of international laws and borders by other nations, including the United States, is no small matter. According to Noam Chomsky, the U.S. defense of high principles can be summed up as follows:

- The U.S. invasion of Grenada
- The U.S. invasion of Panama, where the United States installed a puppet regime of its choice with U.S. military advisors running it at every level.
- The U.S. mining of the Nicaraguan harbor. The World Court finds the U.S. guilty and the United States's reaction was to arrogantly dismiss the World Court.
- The Turkish invasion and virtual annexation of northern Cypress that killed a couple hundred people and drove out several thousands. The United States was in favor of the action.
- The Moroccan invasion of the western Sahara, also supported by the United States.
- The Israeli invasion of Lebanon, where the United States vetoed a whole series of resolutions in the Security Council, which was trying to terminate the aggression. In human terms, there were at least 20,000 killed, mostly civilians.
- The Indonesian invasion of East Timor in 1975 where 60,000 people were massacred. The Carter administration provided 90% of the armaments to the invaders.[7]

Against this landscape of violation of international laws and aggression perpetrated by the United States or other countries with the support of the United States, how can we explain the ease with which Bush convinced a supposedly highly literate and civilized citizenry that

Saddam Hussein's invasion of Kuwait was an isolated case of aggression
against a weaker nation and had nothing to do with the historical record?
The inability to link and treat the "clothesline" of the Gulf War had to
do with ideological obstacles that too often obfuscate political clarity.[8]
Jim Gee's book challenges us to develop a more critical literacy along
Freirian lines where, "as knowing subjects (sometimes of existing
knowledge, sometimes of objects to be produced), our relation to
knowable objects cannot be reduced to the objects themselves. We need
to reach a level of comprehension of the complex whole of relations
among objects."[9] In his book, Jim Gee elegantly demonstrates that "to
explicate the 'internal workings' of the 'machine,' and not the uses to
which the machine is put in the world of value conflicts and political
action" is to treat each piece of the "clothesline" separately so as to never
allow us to reach a level of comprehension of the complex whole of
relations among objects. This functions as a form of illiteracy of literacy
in which we develop a high level of literacy in a given discourse while
remaining semiliterate or illiterate in a whole range of other discourses
that constitute the ideological world in which we travel as thinking beings.

In an era in which we are more and more controlled by ever increasing
technological wizardry, ephemeral sound bites, metaphorical manipulations
of language, and prepackaged ideas void of substance, it becomes that much
more urgent to adhere to Jim Gee's posture that we acquire literacies rather
than literacy. Given our preponderance as humans to construct "satisfying
and often self-deceptive 'stories,' stories that often advantage themselves and
their groups," the development of a critical comprehension between the word
semantic field and a more coherent understanding of the world semantic field
is a prerequisite to achieving clarity of reality. According to Freire, only
"through political practice the less coherent sensibility of the world begins
to be surpassed and more rigorous intellectual pursuits give rise to a more
coherent comprehension of the world."[10] Thus, in order to go beyond a mere
word-level reading of reality, we must develop a critical comprehension of
psychological entities such as "memories, beliefs, values, meanings, and so
forth . . . which are actually out in the social world of action and interaction."
We must first read the world—the cultural, social, and political practices that
constitute it—before we can make sense of the word-level description of
reality.

Jim Gee convincingly demonstrates that the reading of the world must
precede the reading of the word. That is to say, to access the true and
total meaning of an entity, we must resort to the cultural practices that
mediate our access to the world semantic field and its interaction with
the word semantic features. Since meaning is, at best, very leaky, we

have to depend on the cultural models that contain the necessary cultural features responsible for "our stories," and "often self-deceptive stories." Let's take the Gulf War again to exemplify how the role of cultural practices not only shapes but also determines and distorts meanings. During the Gulf crisis we were saturated with all sorts of metaphorical manipulations of language facilitated by the electronically controlled images and messages through "the strategic use of doublespeak to disguise from television viewers the extent of the real terror and carnage of the military campaign against Iraq."[11] According to William Lutz, doublespeak "is a language that avoids or shifts responsibility, language that is at variance with its real or purported meaning. It is a language that conceals or prevents thought; rather than extending thought, doublespeak limits it."[12]

The Gulf War coverage represented the production of doublespeak par excellence. The success to which the media used euphemism to misinform and deceive can be seen in the transformation of the horrible carnage of the battlefield into a "theater of operations" where the U.S. citizenry became willfully mesmerized by the near precision zapping of "smart bombs" during the aseptic "surgical strikes." The "theater of operations" positioned viewers to see "human beings become insentient things while weapons become the living actors of war. 'Smart' weapons that have eyes and computer 'brains' make decisions when and where to drop seven and a half tons of bombs, taking away the moral responsibility of the combatants themselves."[13]

The effective outcome of the doublespeak during the Gulf War was not only to give primacy to sophisticated weaponry with its newly acquired human attributes, but it also functioned as a means to dehumanize human beings by removing them from center stage. The preoccupation of reporters and so-called "experts" was to zealously narrate the "accuracy" of the "smart bombs" while showing over and over again Star-Wars-like images of "surgical strikes." What these reporters did not show was the 92.6 percent of the bombs dropped that were not "precision-guided ordinances" and which amounted to roughly 82,000 tons. Even the 7.4 percent of "smart bombs" dropped during the war had a reliability rate between 20 percent and 90 percent.[14] What the American citizenry was less concerned with was the terror of war and the horrible carnage caused by the 82,000 tons of "delivered packages" that ended up as de facto carpet bombings. Then again, the American viewers had already been positioned in a "theater of operations" context as passive observers seduced and fascinated by the wizardry of exciting precision guided missiles. The "theater" overfloweth with computer graphics, night-vision lenses, cruise missiles and, best ever, the replay of the impact of laser guided bombs."[15] Missing from the "theater" center stage were the horrified human faces of tens of thousands of Iraqis, including women and children, who were decimated by the unparalleled bombing "sorties." The American viewers' feelings were structured away from the reality of over 100,000 Iraqi casualties to the degree that the electronic management of the Gulf War vulgarly reduced human suffering and casualties to mere "collateral damage."

In "The Paradox of the Image," Peter McLaren and Rhonda Hammer accurately characterize the Gulf War as "a gaudy sideshow of flags, emblems, and military hardware—a counterfeit democracy produced through media knowledge able to effectively harness the affective currency of popular culture such that the average American's investment in being "American" reached an unparalleled high which has not been approximated since the years surrounding the post-World War II McCarthy hearings."[16] This unparalleled patriotism was cemented by the signifier yellow ribbon which functioned very effectively to suffocate any truly democratic dialogue. The yellow ribbon ideologically structured the Gulf War debate so as to brook no dissent or dialogue. Criticizing the Bush administration's policies was viewed as not supporting the troops. In fact, the yellow ribbon did more to ideologically cage the American mind than all the speeches given by politicians. One could easily argue that the yellow ribbon patriotically tied American minds by making them sufficiently complacent to be complicit with the manufacture of consent for a fabricated war.

The complexity of networks of relations in our present telecratic society is making our sensibilities of the world less and less coherent, leading to a real crisis of democracy, to the extent that the present

propaganda approach to media coverage suggests a systematic and highly political dichotomization in news coverage based on serviceability to important domestic interests. This should be observable in dichotomized choices of story and in the volume and quality of coverage.[17]

This political dichotomization became flagrantly obvious when, on the one hand, George Bush, in a John Waynean style, rallied "civilized" nations to uphold high moral principles against aggression when Saddam Hussein invaded Kuwait. On the other hand, Mr. Bush sheepishly watched and allowed thousands of Kurds, whom he had incited to revolt, to be exterminated by the same forces of aggression. So much for high moral principles. What is at stake here is our ability as democratic citizens and thinking beings to see through the obvious contradictions and discern myth from reality. However, our level of criticity is being rapidly eroded to the degree that "today's cultural and historical events bombard our sensibilities with such exponential speed and frequency, and through a variety of media forms, that our critical comprehension skills have fallen into rapid deterioration."[18] The deterioration of Americans' critical comprehension of the world became self-evident when they instinctively rallied behind the "Pentagon's vacuous military briefings, lists of aircraft types, missions, and losses [that] have become the sterilized equivalent of body counts recited in Saigon. Far more important elements—human and political—are being lost."[19] It is indeed a sad statement about the ability of the American citizenry to make the necessary historical linkages so as to develop a rigorous comprehension of the world when, with the exception of a small minority of others only Vice-President Dan Quayle was able to read the Gulf War reality correctly by describing it as "a stirring victory for the forces of aggression."[20]

Jim Gee's book *The Social Mind* challenges us to overcome this rapid deterioration of our critical comprehension skills as it calls for the institution of critical literacies as a form of cultural politics. That is, the study of the mind, literacies, or for that matter, any field of study, must involve rigorous connectedness so that the "social, cultural, ideological, and political considerations are not at the periphery of the field, they are at the heart of the matter."

DONALDO MACEDO
University of Massachusetts at Boston

NOTES

1. Roger Fowler et al., *Language and Control* (London: Routledge & Kegan Paul, 1979), p. 192.

2. Greg Myers, "Reality, Concensus, and Reform in the Rhetoric of Composition Teaching," *College English* 48, no. 2 (February 1986).

3. Frei Betto, quoted in Paulo Freire & Donaldo Macedo, *Literacy: Reading the Word and the World* (South Hadley, MA: Bergin and Garvey, 1987), p. 13.

4. Ibid., p. 130.

5. Daniel Patrick Moynihan, quoted in Noam Chomsky, "On the Gulf Policy," *Open Magazine*, Pamphlet Series, 1991, p. 8.

6. Ibid., p. 8.

7. Chomsky, "On the Gulf Policy," p. 8.

8. Freire and Macedo, *Literacy: Reading the Word and the World,* p. 131.

9. Ibid., p. 131.

10. Ibid., p. 132.

11. Peter McLaren and Rhonda Hammer, "The Paradox of the Image: Media Knowledge, and the Decline of Quality of Life," in Ivan Simonis (ed.), *Anthropologie et Sociétés*, in press.

12. William Lutz, *Doublespeak* (New York: Harper Collins, 1989), p. 4.

13. Carole E. Cohn (1991), "Decoding Military Doublespeak," ms 1, no. 5 (May 28), p. 88.

14. Paul F. Walker and Eric Stambler, "The Surgical Myth of the Gulf War," *The Boston Globe*, April 16, 1991, p. 15.

15. Editorial, "Packaging the War," *The Boston Globe*, January 20, 1991, p. 18.

16. McLaren and Hammer, "The Paradox of the Image," p. 12.

17. Edward S. Herman and Noam Chomsky, *Manufacturing Consent: The Political Economy of the Mass Media* (New York: Pantheon Books, 1988), p. 35.

18. McLaren and Hammer, "The Paradox of the Image."

19. "Packaging the War," *The Boston Globe*, p. 18.

20. Dan Quayle, *The Boston Globe*, April 12, 1991, p. 15.

INTRODUCTION

In the time during which I have written this book, I have had the stimulating experience of moving back and forth between two quite different worlds. In one world, on the West Coast of the United States, I have worked with a number of colleagues in linguistics and psycholinguistics who believe that what they study has little to do with social values or politics in any sense. They are interested in the *structure* of the mind and the *mechanisms* by which it works. They want to explicate the "internal workings" of the "machine," not the uses to which the machine is put in the world of value conflicts and political action. In the other world, on the East Coast of the United States, I have worked with a number of colleagues who believe that all language, thought, and action is inextricably *social*, *ideological*, and *political*, fully caught up with social values and the workings of power in society.

These two groups, of course, represent a significant divide between a broad range of scholars studying the mind today. On the one side is conventional "cognitive science," a mega-discipline made up of linguists, cognitive psychologists, computer scientists, philosophers of mind, and mathematicians. They study the mind as a system that "carries out" computations (manipulates representations) in much the way a computer, a logician, or a mathematician does. Surely, they will say, we need consider no social or political questions to understand the steps a computer takes to solve a problem or the rules of inference a logician follows to give a proof. So too we need consider no social or political issues to understand the computations of the mind.

On the other side are a more motley array of sociolinguists, social psychologists, anthropologists, philosophers, literary theorists, and educators who view thoughts, words, and actions as processes and products of *social interaction*. For these students of the mind, mind extends beyond the skin to mutually form and be formed by an ever changing physical and social world.

In their more sedate moments (when not competing for grants, raises, and positions), these two groups are liable to claim that there is no real difference of opinion between them. They simply have different emphases and different interests and areas of study.

Cognitive scientists will readily concede that the computational representations they study are put to use in the world in ways that often have social, moral, and political implications. If someone else wants to study these matters, well fine, though such matters (they may claim) are not open to "scientific investigation" in any very "rigorous" way.

On the other hand, social theorists will in all likelihood concede that we each have a brain serving as the basis for a mind that believes, thinks, and remembers in terms of some "mental language" the grammar of which is open to investigation in formal terms. After all (it will be said) one can understand the structure and internal workings of an automobile without touring around the country in it. (You can simply "rev" it up on a static machine and take it nowhere, if you like.)

Perhaps, then, we might say that to a cognitive scientist the most interesting thing about a car is how the machine works, and to a social theorist the most interesting thing about a car is what you do with it and where you take it. That's all there is to it, and you can study what you want. It's a matter of "taste" and your views about what constitutes "science."

No such thing, I believe, is true. If the mind were like an automobile, then, indeed, the differences between cognitive scientists and social theorists of the mind would simply represent a divide of emphases, interests and areas of study. However, the mind is not, in fact, like a car or any other machine (including any sort of computer).

Imagine one had a very special sort of car. When it sits in the garage, it looks just like a heap of parts—pieces of engine here and there, half a fender, a bit of a bumper, part of a steering wheel, half an axle, and so forth. Yet when one enters it, and starts to drive, then low and behold, it looks and acts like a full car in every respect.

Thus, only when one is touring around the country in the car does it look and act like a full-functioning car. In this case, we can most certainly study the heap in the garage, but such a study will tell us very little about the car, and what it tells us may be quite misleading. On the other hand, we can study the whole car, which indeed has a mechanical structure and principles of operation. But we will have to conduct this study "on the fly" so to speak, either studying our own car as we drive around in it, or studying other people's cars as they drive around in them (and therefore while we are out driving around to keep up with them). No easy matter in either case.

I believe that the human mind is much more like our very special car than it is like a common everyday automobile. Thus, studies of the mind as a static thing outside its social world, while often quite accurate, make it sound like just what it then is, a rather odd mechanical heap of parts—which it appears to be in its static state—not a full and functioning thing. Of course, we will definitely want to know, of our special car, why it looks like mechanical heaps when it is left alone in the garage, but this question is unlikely to be answerable apart from understanding the full-functioning car first and foremost.

Too often, however, social theorists simply claim that all language, thought, and action is social, ideological, and political, with no real compelling set of arguments that the mind *needs* to be studied on this basis. The reader of such work too often has no real idea, apart from rhetorical flourishes, exactly why everyday cognitive scientists (like psychologists) cannot go about their business as usual, oblivious of any issues about power, desire, and social groups with their interests and conflicts. This book, throughout, is an argument that psychologists cannot, if they want to understand what they claim to want to understand—namely things like meaning, memory, and beliefs—conduct business as usual.

I will argue that meaning and memory, and other so-called "psychological entities," are not *in the brain or the mind* (no matter how one construes these). As paradoxical (for the present) as the claim might seem, "psychological entities" are actually out *in the social world* of action and interaction.

What is in our heads are rich networks of associations, some of which are our biological "gift" ("innate"), and many others of which are built up by our experiences in the physical and social world from birth on. These associations are *cognitive tools* with which we get into and "play" social "games" or, put another way, "act out" social roles. These "games" are always serious matters in which power, status, and solidarity ("social goods") are at stake. The roles we play always involve assuming or acting as if certain sorts of people and things are "right," "normal," or "good" and certain other sorts are "wrong," "marginal," or "bad."

Psychological entities—memories, beliefs, values, meanings, and so forth—are like "strikes" in baseball. It takes a specific action of the body or a machine to "throw a strike," but a strike is not an action of the body or a machine. Rather, a strike is a "thing" (a rather special sort of thing) that requires the integration of an action, a ball, various positions of that ball in space, a playing field, a set of rules, and various people playing certain roles.

So too, a memory, a meaning, or a belief is not an "action" or "state" of the mind or brain. Rather, each is a "thing" (a rather special sort of thing) that requires the integration of actions or words (and states of the mind/brain) with social practices of given groups of people playing certain roles across time and space with various sorts of material props (e.g., books, money, buildings).

There are no strikes outside the *game* of baseball, and the game does not reside in anyone's body; there are no memories, meanings, or beliefs without social practices, and the social practices do not reside in anyone's head. The game and the social practices are in the material and social world.

The idea that what really is in people's heads are rich networks of associations of a certain sort to be explicated in the body of this book is based on a new theory of the mind/brain coming out of cognitive science frequently called "connectionism." Somewhat ironically, perhaps, I will be arguing in this book that this new and promising theory of the mind/brain in cognitive science actually serves as the basis of a social *theory* of mind and meaning. This social theory integrally relates "psychological entities" to social practices, ideologies, and "politics" in the sense of group interactions in which "power" and "social goods" are at stake. As such it calls into deep question "business as usual" in psychology.

I will carry out this argument, in part, by showing that what is in the head according to a connectionist view of the mind/brain is the *wrong sort of thing* to *be* a memory, a meaning, a belief, or other such "psychological entity." It is only the right sort of thing to be the prerequisite for getting into and playing out social practices in much the same way that a body skilled in a certain way is the prerequisite for getting into and staying in a game of baseball. The social practices I refer to each constitute socioculturally different notions of what "count" as memories, meanings, values, and beliefs and the links among these.

The logic of the argument I will develop, however, will still hold even if one rejects a connectionist view of the mind. Its basic force holds that memories, beliefs, values, meanings, and so forth are just simply not things individuals can do alone and in the privacy of their heads, no matter what is going on in those heads. I develop my argument through appeals to a connectionist view of the mind because I believe that such a view of the mind actually makes sense of how the mind/brain relates to the essentially social nature of things like memory, beliefs, values, and meanings.

This book is written by a linguist who wants to communicate to people interested in language and mind from a wide variety of disciplines. Thus, I have attempted to make my argument about the mind and social practices as clear as I possibly can. I have placed the emphasis not on the details, but on the nature of the argument itself. This is a book about the forest, not the trees.

My goal is to persuade the reader that the study of the mind is a study of social practices, which are inherently ideological and political. Psychology is a *social science*. Social, cultural, ideological, and political considerations are not at the periphery of the field; they are the heart of the matter. They are not "add ons" after we have sketched the "grammar of the mind." Without them, the mind/brain is a heap of meaningless mechanical parts (to be properly studied by physicists, chemists and neurobiologists). This heap is not, according to my argument, the subject matter of any viable psychology. On a more positive note, I will attempt to sketch out what I argue is in its own right a viable field of study—a field that studies "psychological entities" out in the material and social world.

The view of language, mind, and society that I take in this book has important implications for human development, education, and the nature of distributive justice in society at large. In the latter part of the book I take up these issues in tandem with the general theoretical discussion. But, more significantly, the theory of language, mind, and society argued for in this book has as one of its chief consequences that any rigid divide between theory and practice, as well between "pure" and "applied" science, in regard to the study of the human mind is illusory.

The organization of the book is as follows: Chapter 1, "Meaning," argues that meaning is not in the head and develops a view of meaning as rooted in "cultural models" (simplified views of the world held by various social groups). Chapter 2, "Mind," introduces a connectionist view of the mind/brain and argues that what is in the mind/brain is not the "right sort of thing" to constitute "psychological entities" like meanings, memories, beliefs, and so forth. Chapter 3, "Memory," discusses one such psychological entity, namely memory. It argues that memory is a social phenomena, not anything in the mind/brain. At the same time, the chapter develops a view of how what *is* in the mind/brain relates to memory.

Chapters 1–3 are background for the overall theory of language, mind, and society that is developed in the following two chapters. Chapter 4, "Soul," is the "heart and soul" of the book. It draws together what has come before and what will come after, sketching out a theory of mind and society and the nature of a socioculturally based psychology. The chapter closes on an argument, using both neuropsychological and evolutionary evidence, that what humans are primarily good at is constructing satisfying and often self-deceptive "stories," stories that often advantage themselves and their groups.

Chapter 5, "Society," offers an explicit view of how language fits within social practices and, thus, offers a view of what a socioculturally situated linguistics would look like. This chapter also discusses some of the educational implications of the viewpoints taken in the book as a whole. The conclusion, "The Social Mind," summarizes claims about the political and ideological nature of social practices through an analysis of a single text.

Some of the material in Chapter 5 reworks, in the framework of the argument developed in the preceding chapters, ideas first developed at length in my book *Social Linguistics and Literacies: Ideology in Discourses* (1990c).

The current book argues that meaning is a matter of words or actions being "recognized" as meaningful in specific ways within the practices of specific social groups. I cannot (at least yet) know what meanings my readers will recognize. However, I can acknowledge my debt to those who have helped me offer the words of this book up for recognition (with or without their agreeing with me).

I am indebted to Donaldo Macedo, who is the editor of the series this book is in as well as a valued colleague and friend. Donaldo asked me to write this book, and has encouraged and helped with the development of these ideas over the course of a number of years.

As always I am indebted to Sarah Michaels, with whom I have worked closely for some time now. For Sarah and me ideas often exist somewhere between us—each of us holding pieces of the whole, neither of us having the whole idea in our own heads.

Reading what Courtney Cazden and Jim Wertsch have written and listening to what they have to say has been (as always) a source of enthusiasm and inspiration.

The people at and around the Literacies Institute (housed at the Educational Development Center in Newton, Massachusetts) have been a fertile source of ideas, and a perfect example of a formative social practice in which theory and practice meld and ideas lie out in the physical and social world for all to share. The President of EDC, Janet Whitlaw, is that rarest of rare things, the perfect administrator: highly intelligent, immensely supportive, and wisely directive. We at the Institute have all benefited immensely from her guidance.

Elaine Anderson, Darsie Bowden, John Gee, Candace Mitchell, Slyvia Sensiper, and Kristine Strand have offered enough help of all sorts as to render obvious the claims this book makes for the social nature of the mind. My copy editor, Wanda Giles, not only substantively improved my writing, but offered insightful comments along the way. Finally, I am indebted to Sophie Craze from Bergin and Garvey who shepherded me and my manuscript at the beginning of the process and to Nina Neimark who did so at the end.

1

MEANING

One of the main themes of this book is that "meaning," "thinking," "memory," "knowledge," and "belief" are not the names of *mental* entities residing privately in people's heads. They are, rather, the names of *socio-mental* practices that extend beyond the skin to include the world and society. In regard to human cognition, the proper unit of study is not, I believe, the individual mind/brain, but people engaged in social forms of life out in the world. I certainly do not deny that humans have heads with brains in them, although I think that we have greatly overrated this fact about ourselves.

Let us start by considering what it is that constitutes the *meaning* of a word. One of the common ways in which meaning is viewed in linguistics, psychology, and philosophy is as follows (e.g., Frege, 1892): The meaning of a word is what allows us to identify something as falling under the *denotation* of that word. The *meaning* of the word "cat," for instance, is "what allows me to know whether something is or is not a cat." While there are intense debates about what exactly this "what" is, standard accounts in linguistics, psychology, and philosophy (Mandler, 1984; Miller & Johnson-Laird, 1976; Saussure, 1916) take it to be a mental entity: my concept of a cat, or information I have stored in my head about cats, or a prototype image of a cat, and so on and so forth through a variety of other suggestions.

The traditional theory is that there is *something* in my head (a concept, a mental representation, images, what have you) that just *is* the meaning of the word "cat," and this something is similar enough to what is in other people's heads (provided that they speak the same language) to (usually) ensure the success of communication. This theory is not only one that has been prevalent in philosophy, psychology, and linguistics for centuries, it is also, in fact, our "folk (common sense, everyday) theory" of meaning.

This folk theory of meaning is riddled with problems. It works poorly for words like "cat," and is a complete nonstarter for words like "justice," "love," "honesty," "poetry," "democracy," and so on (which usually, for some reason, play no role in accounts of word meaning in linguistics and philosophy). To see the beginnings of the problem here, but only the beginnings, I want to consider my own version of a well-worn argument first developed by the philosopher Hilary Putnam (1975). Putnam's point in using the argument was to show that meaning is *not* a matter of having one's mind/brain in the right (mental or neurophysiological) state; indeed, his point was that meaning is not in the head at all, but in the world. This, however, will only be a part of my point, not the whole of it.

The argument is essentially a thought experiment. To begin the argument, we first make a number of assumptions. Imagine that we have identical twins separated at birth named Joe and Fred. Joe lives on earth. Fred lives on a planet called "twin earth." Twin earth looks in every regard just like earth. There is, however, one difference between earth and twin earth, though you can't see it. On earth, *water* is H_2O, and on twin earth, while the stuff called "water" is qualitatively identical in every respect (looks and tastes the same, and so forth), it is XYZ, a chemical difference irrelevant to all daily macroscopic water phenomena.

Joe from earth goes to visit his brother Fred on twin earth, bringing with him some food and water for his journey. Now assume that, as Joe and Fred stand in front of a twin earth lake, their heads just happen to be in exactly the same neurophysiological states (assume, indeed, that their brains are in physically and functionally identical states, however one wants to determine that). What's going on in their heads is the same at the moment. We make this assumption because we are now going to have them utter exactly the same words. Since their heads are, by assumption, in the same states and they will have said exactly the same thing, then, *if meaning is a matter of what is going on in their heads*, their words should mean exactly the same thing when they utter them (since their heads are the same, by assumption).

Now imagine that both Joe and Fred point to the twin earth "lake" they are standing in front of and simultaneously say, "There is water in that lake." We will assume that neither Joe nor Fred knows anything much about chemistry, and, in particular, neither one happens to know the chemical composition of "water." We now reach our key question: Do Joe and Fred mean the same thing by their words "There is water in the lake"?

Some philosophers hold that the meaning of an utterance, whatever and wherever it is, determines the conditions under which the utterance is true or false. If that is your view of the matter, then consider the fact that the utterance "There is water in that lake" is made true or false on twin earth by the presence or absence of XYZ, while a similar utterance about a lake on earth is made true or false by the presence or absence of H_2O. So *if* meaning determines truth conditions, then meaning can't be fully explained simply by reference to the states of people's heads. This is so because Joe's and Fred's heads are in the same states, but they cannot mean the same thing by "There is water in the lake," this being made true or false by the presence of H_2O for Joe and by the presence of XYZ for Fred. Since their utterances are made true or false under different conditions, they cannot mean the same thing, despite the fact that their heads are the same in all requisite regards.

Notice that this argument works even if it is empirically true that no two heads could actually be in the same state at the same time when two people are uttering claims, since it shows that the assumptions we make about what's going on in their heads, whatever they are, don't affect what we say about their meanings.

Other philosophers hold that the meaning of an utterance determines the ways in which we would argue for or against the truth of the utterance, that is, the ways in which we would defend a claim to know that the utterance was true. In this view, meaning isn't still in the head. Imagine that someone else, say Mary, a person from twin earth, comes along and challenges the statements made by Joe and Fred. Mary claims to be a chemist and claims also to have traveled to earth. She says, "I'm a chemist and I think you are both wrong. That stuff out there isn't what I've seen on earth, and it isn't what I've seen in other twin earth lakes either—it's something else altogether." Mary has thus challenged the truth of what both Joe and Fred have said, and they must defend it. Since they have said the same thing, and their mind/brains are in the same states, they should both win or lose their challenge together (if meaning is in the head). But this is not what will happen.

What will Joe and Fred do? Well, if pushed far enough by the challenge, they will take the stuff in the lake to an independent chemist and have it "checked." But what does that involve? Well, consider first Joe from earth. He takes a sample of the water he brought from earth (which he trusts is water) and gives the sample to the chemist, along with a sample from the twin earth lake, and asks the chemist to tell him whether the two samples are the same stuff. And, of course, the chemist says "No, they are not." (So Mary wins the challenge in this case.) And now consider what Fred from twin earth does. He takes a sample that he is sure is water—perhaps a previous chemist checked it for him—gives it to the same chemist Joe used (to be fair), together with a sample from the lake, and asks the chemist to tell him whether the two samples are the same stuff. And now, of course, the chemist says, "Yes, they are the same." (Mary was either fooling or just plain wrong in this case.)

So Joe and Fred have said the same thing, and their heads are in the same states, but one turns out to be wrong and the other correct; one uttered a true sentence and the other a false one. Further, one has won and one has lost his challenge to Mary. The sentences they have uttered cannot therefore mean the same thing. Since by assumption, their heads are in the same states and they have uttered the same words, nothing in their heads or words could have determined the meaning difference in the utterances. What determined the truth or falsity of their statements, or their abilities to defend their statements, were *states of the world* (earth having H_2O and twin earth having XYZ). In Putnam's well-chosen phrase: "meaning just ain't in the head."

This sort of argument has caused a great deal of controversy in philosophy. But it shows, at the very least, that the way the *world* is, (the world in which we originally learned and continue to use our language) determines, at least in part, what a word means. Many formal semanticists (e.g., Cresswell, 1990, 395) share Putnam's view to the extent that they think of meaning as a relationship between *language* (for example, the word "water") and the *world* (that is, water, which is H_2O on earth), not between *minds* (e.g., someone's concept of water) and the world.

Now we part company with Putnam. Part of what makes the earth/twin earth argument compelling is that all of *us* would cease to think of something as water if we found out it wasn't H_2O (or, at least, found out that the stuff in front of us didn't have the same internal structure as the other instances of water around us), even if it looked and felt like water. Words like "water," "tiger," and "gold" are called "natural kind terms." They name things that have a characteristic internal structure (whether chemical or genetic). Just as in the case of water, if we found out that something that looked and acted like a tiger had a very different genetic structure from typical tigers, we would no longer think it was a tiger.

Now, why are we so willing to forego the appearances of these things and give up our claim that something is water or a tiger if we discover that its internal structure is not the same as it is in other typical instances? The reason is that we all share the viewpoint that things like water, tigers, and gold have a characteristic internal structure that determines that they are water, tigers, and gold. And we hold this view even if we don't know, or no one in fact knows, exactly what that internal structure is. This viewpoint we all share is really a tacit *theory*, a theory about the relationships between words like "water," "gold," and "tiger" (natural kind terms) and things like water, gold, and tigers in the world. The theory stands between (mediates between) the words and the world. Let me call such theories "semantic mediational theories." I promise to get rid of this ugly piece of jargon relatively soon.

Such a semantic mediational theory as we have for natural kind terms like "gold" and "water" is by no means necessary. Others are perfectly possible. We can certainly imagine a group of people that considered the appearances and functions of things like water, gold, and tigers as of paramount importance, and who accepted accounts of casual efficacy that sometimes referred to outside, nonmechanical forces (for example, gods or spirits). If such people were told that a lump of gold had changed its internal structure, but that this had no implications for its appearances or uses, then they might well say that someone or something had changed their lump of gold, but they would mean by this not that it had ceased to be gold but only that it had changed in one of its nonessential properties, namely, its internal structure, which for us is the essential property of gold sine qua non.[1]

Of course, philosophers will say that these people are not treating "gold" as a natural kind term and don't mean by "gold" what we do. And that is fine, as far as I am concerned. All I claim is that they have a different semantic mediational theory, and claiming that their having a different theory causes them to have a different meaning simply supports my contention that the semantic mediational theory is relevant to what meaning is (Hacking, 1986). The crucial question is what these semantic mediational theories are and where they reside (in the head, in the world, in both, in neither?).

SEMANTIC MEDIATIONAL THEORIES

Now I want to get at what and where these semantic mediational theories are. To begin to answer these questions, let us turn our attention to a word which is not a natural kind term, namely the word "bachelor." This word is one of the rather rare ones in the language that appears to have a perfectly straightforward definition: *unmarried male* (*Webster Handy College Dictionary*, 1972).

But now let me ask you: Is the pope a bachelor? Is a thrice-divorced man a bachelor? Is a young man who has been in an irreversible coma since childhood a bachelor? What about a eunuch? A committed gay man? An elderly senile man who has never been married? The answer to all these questions is either "no" or "I'm not sure" (as I have discovered by asking a variety of people). Why? After all, all these people are unmarried men.

The reason that the answer to these questions is "no," despite the fact that they all involve cases of clearly unmarried males, is that the word "bachelor," just like the word "water," is connected to a theory, a semantic mediational theory. One way to look at semantic mediational theories is as *models of simplified worlds*. For example, our semantic mediational theory for natural kind terms involves a model of the world in which each thing in the world has a characteristic internal structure that renders it that kind of thing. This is actually not the way the "real" world works. In the "real" world some things have quite ambiguous internal structures that render decisions about kinds hard to make. There are, for example, various hybrids and genetic anomalies—for instance, there are humans with anomalous genetic structures that make it very hard to say whether they are females or males (Churchland, 1986, 88–97; Fausto-Sterling, 1985; Laqueur, 1990).

Furthermore, what counts as a relevant internal structure is always a *theoretical* matter, not a simple "fact." For example, should we count the "spin" or "handedness" of atoms as relevant to the internal structure of the kinds of things we recognize? If we did, perhaps some water and tigers would then differ from others. Thus, our semantic mediational theory about natural kinds is in fact a model of a simplified world, abstracting away from complexities in the real world. Of course, all theories, including scientific theories (Holton, 1988), are this way, not just semantic mediational theories.

What, then, is our semantic mediational theory for "bachelor," and how does this theory relate to the fact that we are reluctant to call the pope a bachelor despite the fact that he is an unmarried man? In our culture, the semantic mediational theory for the word "bachelor" is something like the following (Fillmore, 1975; Quinn & Holland, 1987): "Men marry women (not other men) at a certain age; marriages are meant to last for life; and in such a world, a bachelor is a man who stays unmarried beyond the usual age, thereby becoming eminently marriageable" (Quinn and Holland, 1987: 23).

We know that this simplified world is not always true, just as we may know that the simplified world described by our semantic mediational theory for natural kind terms is not always true, but it is the one against which we use the word "bachelor." Thus, the reason the pope is not a bachelor is because he just isn't in this simplified world, being someone who has vowed not to marry at any age. Nor are gay men, since they have chosen not to marry women.

The example of the semantic mediational theory attached to "bachelor" brings out a crucially important property of semantic mediational theories in general. Semantic mediational theories have the property of "marginalizing" certain experiences, certain things, or certain people; that is, they define certain experiences, things, or people as noncentral, abnormal, or otherwise anomalous. Semantic mediational theories involve us in exclusions that are not at first obvious and which we are often quite unaware of making. The semantic mediational theory for "bachelor" assumes that men come in two "normal" types: those who get married early and those that get married late. This assumption treats gays and priests and people who otherwise don't want to get married as non-normal; such men are not "central cases" of men.

There is even a more subtle exclusion being made via this semantic mediational theory. If men become "eminently marriageable" when they stay unmarried beyond the usual age, this can only be because we have assumed that after that age there is a shortage of "desirable" men and a surplus of women who want them, women who, thus, aren't "eminently marriageable," or, at least, not as "eminently marriageable" as the men. Thus, women who "stay unmarried beyond the usual age" are not "eminently marriageable," and, hence, we get the semantic mediational theory associated with "spinster."

Now this marginalization process is quite normal with semantic mediational theories. For instance, the semantic mediational theory connected with natural kind words marginalizes (defines as noncentral cases) hybrids and genetic anomalies (note, for example, the effect this has had on folk theories about keeping blood "pure" and not mixing "races"). Furthermore, it assumes that people who are in a position to discover the internal structure of things like water, tigers, and gold—namely, scientists—are more centrally placed in relation to the meaning of these words than are others. In this respect they are "experts" and the rest of us are "amateurs," even in regard to the most common elements of our world. Finally, it marginalizes "appearances" (the look, feel, taste, and function of water, for instance) as against invisible "underlying structure."

The ways in which semantic mediational theories set up central and marginal cases, hierarchies of experiences, things, and people, renders them inherently *ideological*. By "ideology" I mean any theory that involves assumptions (however tacit they may be) about the "value" (prestige, power, desirability, centrality) of experiences, things, or people (Fairclough, 1989; Gee, 1990c). Again, this ideological component to semantic mediational theories is not an "add on;" it is a normal and central property that they have. Note that my theory of semantic mediational theories (using the words "normal" and "central") is, of course, itself ideological. Having gotten a sense of what semantic mediational theories are, we can now directly take on the question of where they are. We do so in the next section.

CULTURAL MODELS

Anthropologists often refer to what I have called a "semantic mediational theory" as a type of *cultural model* (Holland & Quinn, 1987).[2] I will now dispense with the cumbersome jargonistic phrase "semantic mediational theory" in favor of the better-sounding term "cultural model." Semantic mediational theories are merely cultural models of the relationship between a given word or type of word and the world (the world as the culture sees it).

In order to get at the question as to where cultural models are (and, specifically, whether they are in our heads), I want to consider a fascinating study by Dorothy Holland and Debra Skinner (1987). They studied the ways in which college-age females think about close male-female relationships. They found there was a standard, taken-for-granted way in which college-age women view close male-female relationships— both romantic and friendly—as coming about. This "cultural model" works something like the following, to quote Holland and Skinner's work (101–2):

College-Age Female's Cultural Model for Close Male-Female Relationships

The male demonstrates his appreciation of the female's personal qualities and accomplishments by concerning himself with her needs and wants, and she, in turn, acts on her attraction to him by permitting a close, intimate relationship and by openly expressing her admiration and affection for him. In the prototypical relationship, the two parties are equally attractive and equally attracted to one another. However, if the discrepancy in relative attractiveness is not great, adjustments are possible. A relatively unattractive male can compensate for his lesser standing by making extraordinary efforts to treat the woman well and make her happy. A relatively unattractive female can compensate by scaling down her expectations of good treatment.

Now it turns out that college-age women label males in terms of this simplified model. It is particularly interesting to note that they have a rich set of labels for males who threaten the model in some way. One class of such males are males who are attractive or popular with women and who are arrogant and self-centered about it. Such males may take advantage of their attractiveness to women to gain affection and intimacy without having to give back the friendship or caring that would normally follow mutual attraction in the simplified, taken-for-granted world given above. Their attractiveness may cause the woman to reveal her affection and admiration for the male without getting good treatment in return. She will then seem less attractive than the male, in turn lowering her prestige as a partner. Such men get such labels as "Don Juans," "jocks," "chauvinists," "hunks," "studs," and "playboys," terms often, though not always, used as insults.

In contrast to the above type of problematic male, there are the males who are not attractive to females and who are not adept at pleasing them. Unattractive males of this type are problematic because they pursue a female who is more attractive than they are. Since they are not only unattractive but also inept at pleasing the female by treating her well, they have no chance of success. Yet they are often unaware of this and unaware that the female is more attractive than they are. Thus, they may hang around and become an embarrassment, lowering the woman's prestige and forcing her to treat them badly. Such males are labeled by such terms as "jerks," "turkeys," "nerds," and "wimps," all and always terms of insult.

Here, once again, we see that a cultural model not only defines what is normal and to be expected but also sets up what counts as non-normal and threatening. One can understand the labels for problematic males only against the taken-for-granted cultural model the women have for the ways that close male-female relationships come about. Even people who would consciously disown many aspects of the value system behind this model readily and unconsciously engage in it in their daily lives. There is a price for not doing so. You become problematic vis-à-vis the taken-for-granted model, in danger of being labeled by some term of insult reserved for the non-normal.

This cultural model also exemplifies another common property of many such models. Very often, despite the fact that such cultural models may have quite drastic impact on people's lives and self-images, they appear to us to be "trivial," not worth study or serious concern. This, of course, simply protects them from change and privileges those who are not marginalized by the cultural model, as does the fact that questioning the model, or refusing to behave in terms of it, opens one up to being marginalized by it and thus dismissed.

Now, we have come some ways from water and bachelors to jerks and jocks, but Holland and Skinner's study allows us to raise the question as to where the cultural model they uncovered resides. Is it in the heads of these women? The answer, as far as I am concerned, is: it could not matter less *what* is in their heads (though I will take up the question as to what *is* in their heads in the next chapter). These young women engage in a specific "*social practice*," a practice which involves dating certain people and not others, responding to certain people in certain ways, talking about them in certain ways, acting and looking certain ways in certain settings, and calling certain people "jerks" and others "studs" in particular settings.

Imagine a young woman named Mary Jane. Mary Jane is a member of this practice, and she calls just the right people "jerk" in just the right settings, while carrying out the rest of the social practice in recognizably acceptable ways. If we were to find out that Mary Jane had no clear conscious or unconscious idea about the cultural model underlying the practice, or, for that matter, had nothing particularly relevant to the model going on in her head (say we determined this by sophisticated neurophysiological tests), we would still conclude that she successfully calls people "jerk." What Mary Jane says when she says "jerk" most certainly *means jerk*, and she could not point to our fancy neurophysiological tests to exonerate herself, should she want to exonerate herself. In this setting, within this social practice, if you pull off enough performances in the right way, you count as a member of the practice and your calling someone a "jerk" means you *think* they're a jerk, even though you may at the time be thinking nothing. Once you are a member of the group, once your behaviors count as meaningful within the social practice, you get the meanings "free."

There is another way to see the same point. Imagine someone says (falsely) to Mary Jane, "You don't know what the word *jerk* means." How can Mary Jane defend herself? Certainly not by looking in a dictionary. Even though "jerk" is in the dictionary, a dictionary would not work. The only way to settle a dispute about whether you know the meaning of a word is to show that you know how to *use* the word "correctly," and dictionaries can't settle disputes about use. For example, a child asked to produce a sentence from the following definition of "redress"—"1. set right; repair; remedy: *King Arthur tried to redress wrongs in his kingdom*"—gave the sentence: "The *redress* for getting well when you're sick is to stay in bed" (Adams, 1990, 147). So much for dictionaries and the use of words.

Mary Jane cannot defend herself either by using fancy new neurophysiological tests to show that what was going on in her head was the "same" as what was going on when others in her group used "jerk," not at least if she continually called the leading stud a jerk. She *could*, however, line up a hundred men and pick out the jerks. If her judgments agreed pretty much with the judgments of the other members of her group, then, sooner or later, we (and they) would conclude that indeed she knew what the word "jerk" meant (within her social practice), regardless of what went on in her head when she said the word (this is, of course, just a variant of Wittgenstein's (1958) famous "beetle in the box" argument).

Let me just point out, without further elaboration here, that in this discussion about meaning not being in the head, I have alluded to claims like "Mary Jane *thinks* someone is a jerk when she calls him a 'jerk' " and "Mary Jane *knows* what the word 'jerk' means," where these claims have in them words that we typically think of as *mental terms*, that is, terms for things going on in heads, namely, "think" and "know." But since Mary Jane could perfectly well be said to know what the word "jerk" means or to think someone is a "jerk" when she is getting the social practice *consistently* right, regardless of what is going on in her head, then "know" and "think" cannot really be naming things going in heads either.

In fact, "know" and "think" are connected to our cultural model of the mind (D'Andrade, 1987), which *treats* them as things going on in the head. But this cultural model (actually a part of our cultural model of the mind), like all cultural models, exists within certain social practices and need not be in the mind in any very specific way, or, at least, we need make no assumptions about how it is in the mind in order to successfully carry out the practice and successfully use the words "know" and "think" so as to "prove" we know what they mean. Though this may seem paradoxical, I will take up the matter directly in Chapter 3, where the air of paradoxicality will be removed.

So where have we got? The meaning of a word is what allows one to identify something as falling under the denotation of the word. And what allows us to count as having successfully identified something as falling under the denotation of a word, what allows us to count as having successfully identified something or someone as water, a bachelor, or a jerk, is a *cultural model* that resides in a given *social practice*. The cultural model resides within the social practice in the sense that we can *induce* what the model is by observing the practice (as Holland and Skinner did for the women they studied). However, no one in the practice *need* have the cultural model in his or her head, consciously or unconsciously, in full or in part. Or, at least, we do not need to make assumptions about what is going on in their heads to make sense of the practice, nor do people in the practice need to check assumptions about what is going on privately in people's heads in order to get on with the practice.

To see more clearly what I am claiming, consider the way in which people move around a city. Some people undoubtedly have quite impressive "maps" of the city in the heads, others have less complete ones, and some people have quite impoverished ones. However, people do not *need* to have any very full representations in their minds of the city, since the structure of the city, out in the world as it is, determines a good deal of their movement (and interactions with each other as well) in and of itself (Jackson, 1989; Soja, 1988). People's "knowledge" of the city is stored, in good part, out in the city itself. Their "city schema," if we want to talk in psychological terms (Mandler, 1984), is not just made up of things in their heads, it is also composed of the structures in the city itself, as well as physical maps (and things like public transportation schedules) that people can read.

The next chapter will take up the issue of what contributions people's heads *do* make. However, since social practices, and the cultural models they imply, are out in the world, like cities, they "store" meaning as effectively as heads could. The meaning of "bachelor" is a relationship between social dialects of the English language (which transcend individuals) and social practices (which also transcend individuals). Just as we walk around cities, we "talk around" social practices, and in the act *mean*.

The study of meaning is not, then, the study of heads; it is the study of social practices. In Chapter 3, I will make the more paradoxical claim that the study of the mind is not the study of heads, but *also* the study of social practices. As paradoxical as this claim may sound, it really follows, in fact, from the social nature of meaning. But I will leave that until Chapter 3. I want now to turn to meaning beyond simple words and the ways in which people get meanings "free" in becoming accomplished members of social practices.

MEANING BEYOND WORDS: INTERPRETATION

Thus far, we have discussed the meanings of words. But people also talk about the meanings of whole texts, for example, poems, essays, stories, descriptions, and the warnings on aspirin bottles. What is the nature of such meaning? Now, it is an interesting thing about a text that to give its meaning, one has to produce, either out loud or "in one's head," *another text*, where this other text is one's spoken interpretation of the original text or the mental representation of the original text one has stored in one's head. This second text is a *translation* of the first text into a "language" (our "own words" or our mental representation) that we take to somehow give the meaning of the first text.

But this appears to be quite paradoxical. Why would our "translation" of one text into another be a better representation of the first text's meaning than the text already was all by itself? But, of course, the original text was nothing all by itself until we interpreted it, that is, translated it into another text. And what would give the meaning of *that* (second) text, the interpretation? Only another translation, and so on infinitely. This is the paradox of interpretation, that is, that an interpretation of a text is always just another text in "other words," in another language, or in some mental representation (Bakhtin, 1981, 1986; Barthes, 1968, 1975; Derrida, 1976; Fish, 1980; Jameson, 1981; Ricoeur, 1981; Said, 1983; Voloshinov, 1930).

This paradox deepens when we note that the translations people offer for a text (their interpretations) are often different than those other people offer, even when all speak the same language (Bleich, 1978; Willinsky, 1990). Furthermore, the translation any one person offers can differ from time to time and from context to context (Bartlett, 1932; Garnham, 1985). Take, for example, the warning on a Tylenol bottle:

WARNING: Keep this and all medication out of the reach of children. As with any drug, if you are pregnant or nursing a baby, seek the advice of a health professional before using this product. In the case of accidental overdosage, contact a physician or poison control center immediately.

Consider the last line. What does it mean? At certain times and in certain contexts I translate it pretty much into itself. That is, "In the case of accidental overdosage, contact a physician or poison control center immediately" means *in the case of accidental overdosage, contact a physician or poison control center immediately* (where the italic portion is meant to represent some mental representation of the meanings of these words in my mind). At other times, and in other contexts, I worry over that modifier "accidentally" and about the pseudo-Latinate "overdosage" rather than the straightforward fine word "overdose," and translate the line as something more like: someone who thinks he's being "official" (and officious) with that "overdosage," and who wants me not to focus on the seamier side of purposeful drug abuse and fatal overdoses is giving me a legalistic warning that if I get hurt using this drug, even through no fault of my own, his company will not be held responsible, and I had better rely on the medical profession and not the legal one to help me.

Now, some would want to say that only the first of these is the meaning of this text; they would call it the text's "literal" meaning and claim that the second interpretation is some "deeper" interpretive "reading." But the point I want to stress is that both translations (and other possible ones) *follow certain procedures or abide by certain interpretive practices*. The first interpretation treats the language of the warning as "literal language," thus using just one interpretive practice among many, and the other treats it in a different way.

The "literal" interpretation is, like all social practices, subject to variation across groups and to changes across time: for example, different groups relate a word like "immediately" to quite different cultural conceptions of time. Furthermore, among different groups and at different times, what counts as a "literal" (unfancy) interpretation is different (Connerton, 1989), just as what counts as "ordinary," "common," "everyday" reality differs (Callinicos, 1988; Douglas, 1986; Foucault, 1972; Giddens, 1990; also Lave, 1988; Rogoff & Lave, 1984). How do we know whether to treat a piece of language one way (as "literal," for example) or another? Only by adopting a particular convention and following this convention in our method of carrying out our translation. The crucial elements are these interpretive practices and how we acquire them.

What I am suggesting is this: a text has a certain structure (certain words, a certain syntax, and, if spoken, a certain prosody; its words fall into certain patterns within sentences and across the text as a whole). These structural factors of the text set up *"cues."* These cues can be used, in different ways, to produce different translations, within different interpretive practices, practices connected with particular groups of people (for example, lawyers, consumers, family members, teachers, and students in a composition class, Afro-Americans, and so on).

Furthermore, certain cues resonate with certain interpretive practices in particularly salient ways in the sense that these cues particularly invite certain sorts of interpretive practices to operate on them. Thus, I am claiming that the meaning of a text is the potential it has to be interpreted in certain ways by different interpretive practices, where to describe this potential requires a description of particular interpretive practices as well as the cues in the text and the ways in which they resonate with particular interpretive practices.

To exemplify my point, and to follow out some of its implications, I want to consider one particular text that brings out the issues in a clear way. A few years ago I was lecturing to a graduate class, discussing literature. The topic of the "sympathetic fallacy" came up. This occurs when a poem or story treats natural events (say, sunshine or storms) as if they reflected or were "in harmony" with or "in step" with (sympathetic with) human events and emotions. This device has been popular throughout the history of literature and is not uncommon in movies as well. In a production of *Macbeth*, for example, when the sky storms forth thunder and lightning as Macbeth strikes in the dagger, becoming a murderer, there appears to be a confluence between, or a "natural fit" between, human affairs and nature (nature is condemning Macbeth's deed; the deed is "unnatural," not just a legal or conventional violation of the social order).

One function the sympathetic fallacy appears to play in literature is to equate the world of nature (the macrocosm) with the world of human affairs (the microcosm) as it is depicted in a particular work of art (Abrams, 1953). It also suggests that these human affairs, as they are depicted in the work of literary art, are "natural," part of the logic of the universe, rather than conventional, historical, cultural, or class based (Eagleton, 1983, 1984, 1990).

The sympathetic fallacy is one device, among many, that resonates with particular interpretive practices, practices found in literary art and in the mythic systems of many cultures. After I had talked about these matters in class, a graduate student came up to me after class and told me that her five-year-old daughter had used such a device in constructing a "literary" version of events that had transpired at the little girl's recent birthday party.

The graduate student went on to say that she had just read a short story that had clearly engaged in the sympathetic fallacy, and this and the class session had lead her to see "what her daughter's story meant." This last phrase is telling: what it means is that she had seen, not *the* meaning of her daughter's story, but that the story had the *potential* to have a particular interpretive procedure apply to it—in fact, that it positively *invited* this interpretive procedure.

The little girl's story is reprinted below; although it was orginally an oral story, I have presented it in terms of its lines and stanzas, to make clear its "literary" structure (Gee, 1989a:14–15):

How the Friends Got Unfriend

Stanza One (Introduction)

1. This is a story
2. About some kids who were once friends
3. But got into a big fight
4. And were not

Stanza Two (Frame: Signaling of Genre)

5. You can read along in your storybook
6. I'm gonna read aloud

[Story-reading prosody from now on.]

Stanza Three (Title)

7. "How the Friends Got Unfriend"

Stanza Four (Setting: Introduction of Characters)

8. Once upon a time there was three boys 'n three girls
9. They were named Betty Lou, Pallis, and Parshin, were the girls
10. And Michael, Jason, and Aaron were the boys
11. They were friends

Stanza Five (Problem: Sex Differences)

12. The boys would play Transformers
13. And the girls would play Cabbage Patches

Stanza Six (Crisis: Fight)

14. But then one day they got into a fight on who would be which team
15. It was a very bad fight
16. They were punching
17. And they were pulling
18. And they were banging

Stanza Seven (Resolution 1: Storm)

19. Then all of a sudden the sky turned dark
20. The rain began to fall
21. There was lightning going on
22. And they were not friends

Stanza Eight (Resolution 2: Mothers Punish)

23. Then um the mothers came shooting out 'n saying
24. "What are you punching for?

25. You are going to be punished for a whole year"

Stanza Nine (Frame)

26. The end
27. Wasn't it fun reading together?
28. Let's do it again
29. Real soon! (Gee 1989a: 14–15)

The use of the sympathetic fallacy in this story, together with its overall "literary" structure, sets up a field of cues that resonate with certain "literary" interpretive practices. This resonance creates particular interpretations of this text within these interpretive practices—certain interpretations (more than one) are allowed within these interpretive practices, but many are not, because they don't pick up on the cues in the text in the way *these* interpretive practices dictate are appropriate. Thus, let me give you my reading of this text within these interpretive practices (see also, Gee, 1989a, 1990c).

A Reading

The story has an obvious "literary" structure. Note, for example, the introduction in stanza 1, the frame in stanza 2, the title in stanza 3, the start of the story proper in stanza 4, and the closing of the frame in stanza 9. This overall structure shapes the text into the genre of "storybook reading," a genre connected to both "children's literature" and "high literature." Within this genre, devices like the sympathetic fallacy are relevant.

Notice how in the five-year-old's story the sympathetic fallacy is not only used, but is, in fact, the central organizing device in the construction of the story. The fight between the girls and boys in stanza 6 is immediately followed in stanza 7 by the sky turning dark, with lightning flashing, and thence in line 22: "and they were not friends." Finally, in stanza 8, the mothers come on the scene to punish the children for their transgression. The sky is "in tune" or "step" with human happenings.

In the five-year-old's story, the sympathetic fallacy functions in much the same way as it does in "high literature." In particular, the story suggests that gender differences (stanza 4: boy versus girl) are associated with different interests (stanza 5: Transformers versus Cabbage Patches) and that these different interests inevitably lead to conflict when male and female try to be "equal" or sort themselves on other grounds than gender (stanza 6: "a fight on who would be which team"—the fight had been about mixing genders on the teams). The children are punished for transgressing gender lines (stanza 8), but *only after* the use of the sympathetic fallacy (the storm in stanza 7) has suggested that *division by gender,* and the conflicts that transgressing this division lead to, are sanctioned by nature, are "natural" and "inevitable," not merely conventional or constructed in the very act of play itself.

This is one translation (interpretation) of (a part of) this text, following certain interpretive practices. There are others, of course. For example, I have no idea how the mother originally interpreted the text; I only know she must have followed *some* interpretive practice. The cues in this text invite the sort of interpretation I have given above, though this practice could be applied to *any* text (including the aspirin bottle text above); however, some texts would contain far fewer, or less straightforward, cues which resonated less well with this mode of interpretation.

Now, as in the case of words above, I want to raise the issue of *where* the meaning of this text is. Note that we simply need not assume that it is in the daughter's head—she is only five and could not possibly yet "know" the details of the interpretation I have offered. The meaning is in the social practice of interpreting texts in certain ways. The daughter, by placing the cues in the text, gives it a potential to be interpreted in a certain way, whether or not anything is going on in her head, thanks to fact that this interpretive practice *is* going on in the world.

Now one may lodge the following sort of criticism: "What does it matter that this text has this potential? If it is not in the little girl's head, what good does it do her, how can it be her meaning?" In fact, it is very important to see that it can do her a lot of good (and harm), and that it is indeed *her meaning* in a way that this meaning is not available to other children who can't place these cues in their preliteracy texts. To see this, consider how the text came about.

This girl's mother regularly read storybooks to her two young daughters. Her five-year-old had had a birthday party, which had had some problems. In the next few days the five-year-old had told several relatives about the birthday party, presumably reporting the events as a chronologically sequenced set of events in the nature of a "report," without the literary trappings above. A few days later, when the mother was reading a storybook to her other daughter, the five-year-old said she wanted to "read" (she could not yet decode print), and pretended to be reading a book, while telling what happened at her birthday party. Her original attempt at this was not very good, but after a few tries, interspersed with the mother reading to the other girl, the five-year-old eventually produced the story above.

Supported by her mother and sister, the five-year-old is apprenticing herself to a certain social practice, namely, mainstream, school-based "storybook reading." But this social practice is itself an aspect of apprenticeship in another, more mature social practice, namely "literature." Both these practices are integrally connected to certain interpretive practices. This child, when she goes to school to begin her more public apprenticeship into the social practice of literature (or "essayist literacy," for that matter [Scollon & Scollon, 1981]) will look like a "quick study" indeed.

This home-based social practice, with its ways of interacting, talking, thinking, valuing, and reading and its books and other physical props, enables this little girl to form a text of a certain type. And that form invites the operation of the interpretive practices that are part of literary (and school-based) social practices. The little girl gets this meaning free, so to speak—since it is in the world, it need not be (fully) in her head.

Does it do her any good? Indeed, it does: we know that such practices are one of the foundations of the disproportionate success such children have in school, in comparison to many "non-mainstream" children from poorer homes (Adams, 1990; Chall, Jacobs, & Baldwin, 1990). Is it her meaning? Yes: there is a real sense in which she and the other members of her group come to "own" such meanings by controlling such social practices and the social institutions (such as schools) that they are embedded in (Bourdieu, 1977; Bourdieu & Passeron, 1977; Gee, 1990c). She is open to attributions of literary meaning, as well as attributions of intelligence, without our needing to ask what is going on in her head.

However, the meanings her text generates as potential grist for interpretive mills do her some harm as well. The sympathetic fallacy is a double-edged sword. On the one hand, it has been used, from time immemorial, to suggest a deep commonalty between human beings and nature; on the other hand, it has also been used to suggest that "nature" underwrites the hierarchies of power, status, and prestige found at particular times and places within particular cultures.

The little girl's text resonates with a particular ideological message about the distribution of gender roles, a message that may well be against this little girl's own "self-interest" as she grows older and desires to see herself as a whole human, the equal of men. She is already becoming "at home" in certain social practices—in the way in which certain people are quite "at home" in a certain city—which will make her a bearer of meanings in conflict with her own interests within other social practices (for example, women's groups). Just as she is open to attributions of intelligence based on what can be made of her performance by certain interpretive practices, so too she is open to attributions that she as female stands apart, "other," perhaps inferior to men, attributions that have come out of her own mouth ("out of the mouth of babes . . . ").

So with texts, as with words, I have argued that meaning is not in the head, but in *social practices*, social practices that are part of what I will call in later chapters "Discourses" (with a capital "D; see Gee 1990c). Discourses are composed of people, of objects (like books), and of characteristic ways of talking, acting, interacting, thinking, believing, and valuing, and sometimes characteristic ways of writing, reading, and/or interpreting (offering translations of oral and/or written texts sensitive to the cues these texts present for interpretation to these practices). Our little girl's home-based storybook and story-telling practices are part of a Discourse, as are "children's literature," "literature proper," and various school-based literacy and literature practices. In fact, these different Discourses (and others) are, within our society, in collusion with one another in the production of things like school success and "intelligence."

Discourses are out in the world, like books, maps, and cities. Though humans do use their heads (as a matter of empirical fact) when they engage in the social practices that compose Discourses, they don't (logically) need them. If we found out that nothing was going on in our five-year-old's head when she produced her text, provided she continues to produce texts like this, she is going to the head of her class regardless of what goes on in her head. It may (or may not) be an empirical (contingent) fact that she does do certain things in her head (even certain things that other, less "fortunate" children don't do), but the rewards for her labors have nothing to do with what she does in her head, and those rewards are, in another sense of "meaning," the "meaning" of her text.

NOTES

1. For an interesting, extended discussion of natural kind terms, their basis in the innate cognitive endowment of humans and their cross-cultural variation, see Atran, 1990. Atran argues that all cultures, thanks in part to the biological endowment of humans, treat biological kinds (living things such as plants and animals, though not necessarily living things that have been caught up in cultural symbolism, like flowers, for instance) as natural kinds with distinctive "essences" or characteristic (necessary) internal structures. On the other hand, he argues that this is not so for substances (such things as gold and water), which many cultures do not treat as natural kinds. Atran argues that cultures that do treat substances as having characteristic (necessary) essences or internal structures have been influenced by sciences, for example, chemistry and physics. Finally, he argues that modern biology (in counter-distinction

to the common sense of every culture) no longer treats living kinds (species) as characterized by "essences" or fixed internal (genetic) structures, but rather in terms of the roles they play in evolutionary histories. Atran's argument is intricate and controversial, and my discussion here can be made compatible with it by distinguishing between biological kinds (e.g., tigers) and substances (e.g., gold).

2. Throughout this book I will use the terms "cultural model" and "folk theory," which are often used synonymously by anthropologists, in a slightly different way. Imagine we set up a continuum of how much conscious awareness a person has of any given one of her own "theories" or viewpoints. At one extreme end of the continuum the person can articulate a given theory or viewpoint well, and at the other extreme and opposite end of the continuum the person is not at all conscious that she holds a particular viewpoint. There are various points in between these two extreme end points—for example, a person might be able to articulate a particular theory only partly and rather inarticulately, or she might not be able to articulate it at all, though she would be able to acknowledge she holds the theory once it is pointed out to her by someone else that she talks and behaves as if she does, and so forth through many other such intermediary cases. I will reserve the term "folk theory" for cases toward the conscious end of the continuum and the term "cultural model" for cases toward the unconscious end. There are obviously points in the middle of the continuum where it will be indeterminate which term to apply. Further, when I am not concerned with whether someone's theory is conscious or not, or where exactly on the continuum it falls, I will simply use the term "cultural model" as a cover term.

2

MIND

Psychologists and philosophers have always used metaphors to understand the mind (Gardner, 1985; Sternberg, 1990). Until fairly recently,
they have not had very deep access to the internal workings of the brain.
Even with recent advances in neurobiology (P. S. Churchland, 1986),
the physical workings of the brain remain still in many respects a
mystery.

Many modern psychologists and philosophers think of the
"mind/brain" in terms of a metaphorical comparison to a computer,
the mind being the software of the brain's hardware (Allman, 1989;
Johnson, 1991; Johnson-Laird, 1988). In several respects, however,
modern digital computers are not particularly good metaphors for
the mind/brain. Digital computers operate serially, computing one
small step of a problem at a time. The human brain operates in a
massively parallel fashion, carrying out many operations at one and
the same time.

Furthermore, digital computers break down all their operations into
binary decisions (simple yes/no, all-or-nothing decisions). The neurons
in the brain can each be activated to different degrees, depending upon
how greatly they are stimulated by other neurons that send them signals.
They operate more in terms of a scale of how much (lots, little,
somewhere in between) than in terms of simple binary yes/no decisions
(a neuron can "fire" with greater or less frequency; that is, it can fire so
many times per second). However, computer scientists are currently
designing computers that function more like the brain (Allman, 1989;

Johnson & Brown, 1988)—in a highly parallel fashion and with units that can be activated to different degrees, rather than digitally (in terms of discrete yes/no, all-or-nothing decisions).

No matter what sort of computer we metaphorically imagine the mind/brain to be, we still have to say what sort of "symbols" this computer manipulates. And here two metaphors have been common (Johnson-Laird, 1983): pictures (images) and words (language). In the last chapter, I pointed out that the meaning of a word (like "water," "cat," or "honesty") is that in virtue of which we can recognize instances of the "what" the word designates (water, cats, honesty, and so on). What in the mind allows us to pull off such recognitions? Some have said that it is something like pictures or images in the mind, and others have answered that it is something like a language of the mind, a language that bears important similarities to human spoken languages.

Thus, if I know what a cat is, this is taken to mean that, on the image account, I have in my mind something like a picture of a "prototypical" cat, and I compare the cats I see to this mental picture. Provided that they are similar enough, I recognize them as cats. On the language account, what I have in my mind is a description of cats in some sort of mental language with its own words and phrases (which are translatable into English or any other human language). When I see cats, I check them against this description and, provided that they match enough of it closely enough, I recognize them as cats.

There are all sorts of problems with these metaphors, problems that I don't want to go into in any depth here, since I will espouse a different model of the mind. There are breeds of cats with no fur, others with no tail, still others with ears that are plastered onto the top of the heads, and yet others with faces like rats or opossums; cats come in an incredible array of sizes and colors (as big as lions, as small as rats). While an image of a prototypical cat in the mind might account for our feeling that some cats are better representatives of "typical cats" than others, it does nothing to account for the fact that we clearly accept all these cats as cats, regardless of how typical they are or aren't.

Of course, we could have a description of all these possibilities in mind, rather than a picture, or, perhaps, even a set of pictures, rather than a single picture. But, as we saw in the last chapter, even if something fails to fit in any very close way your description or descriptions of a cat, it is still a cat if it has the internal (genetic) structure of a cat, and that is not in your description thanks to the fact that you (and I) don't know it. It is certainly not in any picture either.

Philosophers have debated for centuries as how to characterize concepts like "love", "knowledge," "democracy," "honor," and "beauty;" these don't seem very likely to be images in the mind. In any case, are we to believe that we all have lucid mental pictures or descriptions of these concepts in our minds but that we just cannot dredge them up out of our unconscious minds and so never agree on what they are when we engage in philosophical debate about such terms?

Finally, as Wittgenstein (1958) pointed out, there are many concepts—those named by what he called "family resemblance" terms—for which it is clear that there are no necessary and sufficient features that could occur in a prototypical image nor any necessary and sufficient criteria that could appear in a description. Wittgenstein uses as his example the concept of a "game." Even more than for cats, one can always find a game that contradicts a reputed necessary and sufficient feature or criteria for being a game, and in the case of games there is nothing analogous to genetic structure, the knowledge of which can at least be lodged in someone else's head, to save the day.

There are many attempted answers to these problems. Rather than stay and debate the matter, I want to turn to a relatively new view of the mind, a view that I believe is considerably more promising. This view, which goes under several names—including "connectionism," "neural networks," and "distributed parallel processing"—is inspired by what we know about the way neurons in the brain function, though it is still just a model built around a metaphor (McClelland, Rumelhart, & the PDP Research Group, 1986). Because it uses the brain itself as its metaphor, I believe it gives descriptions of mental processes that are of the right type. I believe that such a model—while it will undoubtedly undergo many and serious changes—will be progressively more and more confirmed in its essential features by ongoing and future work in the cognitive sciences.

A neural network model may well turn out not to be the whole story of the mind/brain. There probably is no single story; the mind/brain may very well operate in several different ways for different purposes. But I believe that it will turn out to be a main and important story about the mind/brain. Furthermore, and this is my central interest in this theory, it allows us ultimately to see that there is much about human mental life that (somewhat paradoxically, perhaps) has nothing much to do with individual minds or brains, but a lot to do with human social practices. In this regard, we will—after a circuitous route—return to where we ended in the preceding chapter.

A CONNECTIONIST ACCOUNT: USING THE
BRAIN AS A METAPHOR FOR THE MIND

The functional atoms of the brain are cells called "neurons." Connectionist approaches to the mind model mental functioning by constructing "networks" of artificial "neuron-like" units. While these artificial neurons are like real neurons in significant respects, they are vastly simpler than real neurons. I will call each simplified artificial neuron in a network, an "artificial neuronal unit," or just a "unit" for short.

Any artificial neuronal unit in a model is connected to a number of other such units by connections (think of them, if you like, as tubes connecting little circles that constitute the units), and these other units are themselves connected to yet other units. A unit sends "signals" (messages) to the other units to which it is connected. The signal a unit sends to other units tells these other units to "fire" (that is, to send *their* signal in turn to other units to which they are connected) or not to fire (not to send their signal to the units to which they are connected).

Actually, things are just a bit more complicated. Any unit can send its signal with different degrees of strength, depending upon how "excited" it is. Furthermore, the connection between any two units always has a certain "size" (or "weight" or "importance"—it doesn't matter which term we use). Any single unit gets signals from lots of other units. The impact a sending unit has on a receiving unit depends on two factors: (1) the *strength* of the signal the sending unit is sending out, and (2) the *weight* (importance) of the connection between the sending unit and the receiving unit (represented by a certain numerical value between 0 and 1). The contribution of a sending unit is just the product of its weight (w_i) times the strength (s_i) of the signal it is sending. A receiving unit determines how strongly to send off its signal to yet other units (the strength of its signal) by considering the sum of the contributions made by all of the units that are sending it signals.

It is as if several friends are yelling a message to me (say, the message "Do it!"). Each friend is yelling with a certain degree of strength (is yelling more or less loudly) depending upon how excited he or she is. Further, each friend has a different connection to me, is more or less important to me in terms of how much I listen to him or her. This is my friend's "weight." The contribution each friend makes to my decision as to what to do (how excited to get, and, thus, how loudly I will yell to other friends) is just the product of how loudly that friend is yelling times how important (weighty) that friend is to me. I decide whether to yell at all to other friends, and how loudly I will yell if I do yell, by summing the contributions of all my friends. If this sum is high enough I yell (if it is not high enough, I don't yell), and the larger the sum, the louder I yell. It is also possible for me to have friends who specialize in yelling not "Do it!" but "Don't do it!" If enough of these sorts of friends are yelling to me—or some very weighty ones are—they can drown out the friends yelling "Do it!" and inhibit my yelling at all.

Thus, units are connected in a network to other units. In the brain, neurons frequently constitute a group, all of which send their connections ("axons") to the site of a second group of neurons, where each arriving connection divides into terminal end branches in order to make connections with many different neurons within the second population. Axons from neurons in this second population can then project to a third population of neurons, and so on. This is the inspiration for the arrangement of units in the network of artificial neuronal units in Figure 2.1 This figure is adapted from Paul M. Churchland's excellent book, *A Neurocomputational Perspective: The Nature of Mind and the Structure of Science* (1989). Much of my discussion in this section and the next is

Figure 2.1
A Simple Network

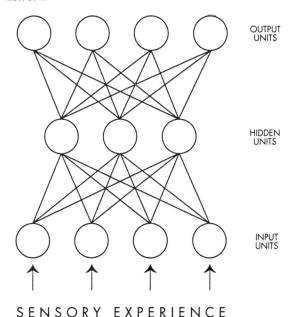

SENSORY EXPERIENCE

Source: This figure is a simplified version of Figure 9.4 in P. M. Churchland, *A Neurocomputational Perspective: The Nature of Mind and the Structure of Science* (Cambridge, Mass.: MIT Press, 1989), p. 162.

based on this work, and on Patricia Smith Churchland's masterful summary, *Neurophilosophy: Toward a Unified Science of the Mind/Brain* (1986).

The units in the bottom or *input* layer of the network may be thought of as "sensory" units, units that experience aspects of the outer world. These units fire off their signals when they sense something in the environment or when the experimenter stimulates them to simulate some aspect of the environment (a sight, a smell, a sound, depending on what we want to model). The strength with which a given unit in the input layer fires is designed to be a response to a specific aspect (feature) of the input stimulus. For example, if some aspect of a given stimulus—say the saltiness of a cracker, if we are modeling taste—is present in a stimulus (for example, a cracker in the real world, or one we are simulating for an artificial network) to a great degree, then a given input unit might fire to a great degree; and if the taste contains only a very small degree of saltiness, then that unit will fire only very weakly or not at all. Other units might respond to other aspects of the taste stimulus (sourness, wetness, grittiness, and the like).

The set of simultaneous levels (strengths) of firing in all of the input units is the network's representation of the input stimulus, its representation of how much of each relevant aspect (saltiness, sweetness, and so on) is present. We may refer to this configuration of stimulation levels as the "input vector," since it is just an ordered set of numbers or magnitudes. For example, a given stimulus might produce the vector $<.5, .3, .9, .2>$, where each number (once again using values between 0 and 1 for convenience) represents the strength with which one of the units in the input layer fires. Thus, in our example vector, the third unit is firing (or is activated) to degree ".9," a great deal—imagine it responds to saltiness and has "sensed" a great deal of it in the cracker. On the other hand, imagine the fourth unit—firing to degree ".2," which is quite weak—picks up on sourness and doesn't find much in this stimulus.

The input units yell (fire off their signals) to the middle layer of the network whose units are called "hidden units." As can be seen in Figure 2.1, any unit in the input layer makes a connection (of a given weight or importance) with every unit at this intermediate layer. Each hidden unit is thus the target of several inputs, one for each unit at the input layer. The resulting strength with which a given hidden unit now fires is essentially determined just by the sum of all of the influences reaching it from the units in the lower, input layer. And the impact of any input unit on a given hidden unit is determined by how excited the input unit is by the environmental stimulus impinging on it (for instances, saltiness for a given input unit or sweetness for another), that is, by the strength of its signal, as well as by the weight (importance) of its connection to the given hidden unit.

In the example above, the third input unit is sending off a strong signal (its value is nearly 1, that is, ".9"), though how much impact this strong signal makes on any given hidden unit to which this third input unit is connected depends also on the weight of its connection to that hidden unit (which amounts to how important its message is for the functioning of that). Imagine, for instance, that our network is meant to recognize that something has the taste of a cracker and a specific hidden unit responds strongly when it receives signals that the stimulus to the input layer is both somewhat salty and flaky in texture (like many crackers), but not too sweet (like some cookies). If input unit 3 responds to the amount of saltiness present in the stimulus, then its connection to this hidden unit might be quite "weighty" (important). Its signal, even when relatively low in strength, encourages this hidden unit to fire (though the unit also "considers" the signals it is getting from all the other input units).

The result of this upward propagation of the input vector is that each hidden unit is "activated" ("excited") to a certain degree and is thus firing off its signal to the next layer with a certain degree of strength. This set of activation levels across the three hidden units in the hidden layer of Figure 2.1 is called the "hidden unit activation vector."

The hidden unit activation vector is in turn propagated upward to the output (topmost) layer of units, where an "output vector" is produced. That is, once again, each unit in the output layer is excited or activated to a certain degree based on all the strengths of the signals being sent to it from all the units to which it is connected at the hidden layer, with due consideration for their various weights. The signals being fired off by the output units are sent, in turn, to some other device (like human muscles or yet other neural networks in the brain, such as one controlling speech) to produce a certain result (for example, the muscle contracts, or the person prepares to say "It's a rather salty cracker").

Looking now at the whole network, we can see that it is just a device for transforming any given input-level activation vector into a uniquely corresponding output-level activation vector, through one or more (one, in the case of Figure 2.1) intermediate levels. The hidden units *mediate* between the world (the effects the world has on the input units) and mental or physical action (the result that the output units cause, whether thoughts, words, or deeds). The hidden units are a "mental" represen-tation of the effects of the world on the input units, a representation that is capable of contributing to further mental activity or activities of the body in the world.

ROCKS AND MINES

This has all been rather schematic, so let me give a concrete example of an artificial neural network that has actually been implemented (Allman, 1989; Gorman & Sejnowski, 1988a, 1988b; see P. M. Church-land, 1989, esp. chap. 9 & 10—my discussion here follows Churchland, 1989). Submarine engineers need sonar systems that can distinguish between the echoes returned from mines and the echoes returned from rocks of comparable sizes that lay in the same underwater terrain. There are two major difficulties in constructing such a device: first, echoes from both objects (mines and rocks) sound indistinguishable to the untrained ear, and second, echoes from each type of thing (mine or rock) vary widely in sonic character, since both rocks and mines come in various sizes, shapes, and orientations relative to the probing sonar pulse.

The artificial neural network shown in Figure 2.2 below is capable of handling this problem. This network has 13 units at the input layer, since we need to code a fairly complex stimulus. A given sonar echo is run through a frequency analyzer and is sampled for its relative energy levels at thirteen different frequencies. These 13 values, expressed as fractions of 1, are then entered as activation levels (strengths of firing) in the respective units of the input layer, as indicated in Figure 2.2 That is, each one of the 13 input units is sensitive to the energy present at a given frequency within a sonar echo; the unit yells out more or less loudly (to the next layer of units), depending upon how much or how little energy exists at that frequency in the sampled sonar echo. The levels of activation across the input layer (the degree to which each unit is firing) constitutes the "input vector."

This input layer signals to the next layer of units—the hidden units—causing each of them to fire to a certain degree and thereby transforming the input vector into a "vector" (set of values or degrees of excitation for each unit) for the hidden layer of units. This layer does the same thing to the next layer. The final result is a pair of activation levels in the two units at the output layer; that is, each one of these units is excited (firing, yelling) to a certain degree. We need only two units here, for we want the network eventually to produce an output activation vector at or near $<1, 0>$ when a mine echo is entered as input (that is, the first unit is firing at a maximal level, namely "1," and the second is not firing, namely, has the value "0"), and an output activation vector at or near

Figure 2.2
The Rock Mine Network

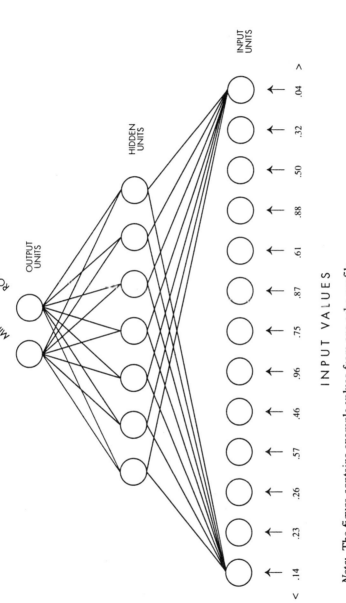

Note: The figure contains example values from one echo profile.

Source: This figure is a simplified version of Figure 9.5 in P. M. Churchland, *A Neurocomputational Perspective: The Nature of Mind and the Structure of Science* (Cambridge, Mass.: MIT Press, 1989), p. 165.

<0, 1> when a rock echo is entered as input (that is, the first unit is not firing, and the second is firing at its maximal level). This amounts to a simple "yes" (<1, 0>), "no" (<0, 1>) response, since we are only interested in whether a mine is present or not. We will see below that the network can also give graded answers like "close to a typical mine, but still somewhat like a typical rock too."

The network, of course, does not start out "knowing" how to tell mines from rocks. It has to be taught to recognize the difference between the sonar echo from a mine and the sonar echo from a rock of comparable size and configuration. This is done by means of the following procedure. We procure a large set of recorded samples of genuine mine echoes, from mines of various sizes and orientations, and a comparable set of genuine rock echoes. We then feed these echoes into the network, one by one, and observe the output vector produced in each case, that is, whether the output layer says "yes, this is a mine" (<1, 0>) or "no, this is not a mine" (<0, 1>) or gives us some value in between (like <.3, .7>, a response leaning toward "no," with .7 as the value of the second output unit, but with still some tendency to say "yes," with a .3 value in the first output unit). Of course, at first, since the network "knows" nothing, the responses will be random and often wrong. What interests us in each trial is the amount by which the actual output vector *differs* from what would have been the correct vector, given the identity of the specific echo that produced it.

For example, say we feed the input layer a genuine mine echo and each input unit responded to whether its given frequency was energetic or not and then signaled to the next (hidden) layer based on this information. The hidden layer, behaving randomly at first, passes certain values to the output layer; say these end up being <.7, .3.>. This is close to saying "yes" (that is, <1, 0>), which is what we want the network ultimately to respond for echoes of this type (since this was a real mine). The details of this error, for each element of the output vector, are then fed into a special mathematical "learning" rule (which we will not discuss here; see Hebb, 1949; Sutton & Barto, 1981) that computes a set of small changes in the values of the various connection weights throughout the network. Thus, perhaps, the rule tells us to make the weight on the connection between input unit 11 and hidden unit 7 a bit "heavier" (more important in the ultimate output determining that something is a mine) and the weight on the connection between input unit 9 and hidden unit 2 a bit "lighter" (less important in determining that something is a mine), and so on.

The idea is to identify those weights most responsible for the error and then to nudge their values in a direction that would at least reduce the amount by which the output vector is in error. The slightly modified network is then fed another echo from the training set, and the entire procedure is repeated. Perhaps this time the response is a bit better (thanks to our earlier modifications of the synaptic weights), and again we modify weights, using our learning rule, and hope to nudge the system toward better and better performances.

Under the pressure of such repeated corrections, the behavior of the network slowly converges on the behavior we desire. That is, after several thousand presentations of recorded echoes and subsequent adjustments, the network starts to give the right answer close to 90 percent of the time. When fed a mine echo, it generally gives something close to a $<1, 0>$ output. And when fed a rock echo, it generally gives something close to a $<0, 1>$. Human sonar operators, after much experience, eventually learn to distinguish the two kinds of echoes with some uncertain, but nontrivial regularity. But they never perform at the level of the artificial network.

So now it looks as though the mine/rock network "knows" the difference between a mine and a rock (or, at least, between a mine echo and a rock echo). In what does this "knowledge" consist? It consists of nothing more than a carefully orchestrated set of connection weights between "neuron-like" units organized into a network (layers communicating to other layers). It is, furthermore, intriguing that there exists a learning algorithm—the rule for adjusting the weights as a function of the error displayed in the output vector—that will eventually produce the required set of weights, given sufficient examples on which to train the network. It could, of course, have happened that there was no way to distinguish between mines and rocks, and, thus, no way to learn how to do so.

How can a set of connection weights possibly embody knowledge of the desired distinction? Think of it in the following way. Each of the thirteen input units represents one aspect (or dimension or feature) of the incoming stimulus (the energy at a given frequency in an echo). Collectively, they give a simultaneous profile of the input echo along thirteen distinct dimensions. Now perhaps there is only one profile of these thirteen dimensions that is roughly characteristic of mine echoes; or perhaps there are many different profiles, united by a common relational feature (for example, that the activation value of input unit 6 is always three times the value of unit 12); or perhaps there is a disjunctive set of such relational features (an example might be that for some mines the activation level of input unit 6 is three times the value of unit 12; for others the activation level of 4 added to the value of unit 12 is twice the value of unit 13; for yet other mines, the value of units 2, 4, and 12 sum to a value below the sum of units 1 and 7); and so forth. In each case, it is possible to rig the weights so that the system will respond in a typical fashion, at the output layer, to all and only the relevant profiles. And there is no need for the relevant profiles (all and only mine echoes) to have anything very elegant or "obvious" or "intuitive" in common (from the point of view of human beings and their opinions about knowledge and science).

The units at the hidden layer are crucial. Imagine that the possible activation levels of the seven hidden units determine an abstract space (P. M. Churchland, 1989: 168–71)—a-seven dimensional space (rather than our typical three-dimensional spaces). Any set of activation values for each of the seven hidden units determines a point in this space, like a location on a seven-dimensional map. What the system is searching for during the training period is a set of weights across the whole network that partitions this seven-dimensional space so that any mine input produces an activation vector across the hidden units that falls somewhere within one large subvolume of this abstract space—one spatial area of the map—while any rock input produces a vector that falls somewhere into the complement of that subvolume, in some area outside the mine "region."

The job of the top half of the network, the output layer, is the now relatively easy one of distinguishing these two subvolumes into which the abstract space has been divided. Hidden unit vectors (a set of activation values for each of the seven hidden units) that land near the center of (or along a certain path in) the mine-vector subvolume represent prototypical mine echoes, and these will produce an output vector very close to the desired $< 1, 0 >$. Hidden unit vectors that land nearer to the surface (strictly speaking, the hypersurface) of the mine-vector subvolume represent atypical or problematic mine echoes, and these produce more ambiguous output vectors, such as $< .6, .4 >$. The network's discriminative responses are thus graded responses: the system is sensitive to similarities along all of the relevant dimensions, and especially to rough conjunctions of these subordinate similarities.

The network is a system that learns to discriminate hard-to-define perceptual features and to be sensitive to similarities of a comparably diffuse but highly relevant character. And once the network is trained, the recognition task—confronted with objects outside the training set—takes only a split second, since the system processes the input stimulus in parallel—it does not consider one frequency value at a time but considers all 13 values at once. The network gives us a discriminatory system that performs somewhat like a living creature, both in terms of speed and in overall character.

The rock/mine network is, of course, much simpler than many other such networks that have been created, since its output is just "yes" or "no" (and so it needs to partition its hidden unit vector space—the values of its seven hidden units—into only two subspaces). Other networks may have a larger number of possible outcomes. For example, a network designed to recognize the letters of the alphabet when fed various types of script and handwriting would have to have 26 outcomes and, thus, would have to partition its hidden unit vector space into 26 subspaces (any set of values across its hidden units would have to fall into one of 26 spaces or regions, each of which represents a given letter, and none of which needs to be very elegant or obvious).

A great many things to which humans respond differentially require people to confront a problem similar to that of telling mine echoes from rock echoes. They are difficult to define or characterize in terms of their purely physical properties but need to be characterized in terms of quite complicated sets of *associations between different features*. Consider, for instance, the vowel in the word "sit," written in phonetic notation as /ɪ/. The range of acoustical variation among acceptable and recognizable /ɪ/'s is enormous. A two-year-old female child and a fifty-year-old male will produce quite different sorts of sound waves in pronouncing this vowel, but each sound will be recognized as an /ɪ/ by other members of the same linguistic community.

While an examination of the acoustical spectrum of vowels reveals some of the similarities that unite all instances of /ɪ/ sounds, there is no simple list of necessary and sufficient physical conditions on being an instance of the vowel /ɪ/. Instead, being an /ɪ/ seems to be a matter of being close enough to a typical /ɪ/ sound along a sufficient number of distinct dimensions of relevance. Each notion in this characterization of what makes a sound an instance of the vowel /ɪ/ is difficult to characterize in a nonarbitrary way. But it is important to see that a "typical" /ɪ/ is not some single "ideal" prototypical /ɪ/, sitting like a picture in one's head, to which all real world /ɪ/'s are compared. Like the case of our rock/mine problem, instances of /ɪ/ cluster in a certain region of acoustic space in virtue of complex associations among the various features that constitute any vowel sound (the energy at different frequencies in the vowel's spectrum, for instance).

Moreover, what constitutes an /I/ is highly contextual. A sound type
that would not normally be counted or recognized as an /I/ may be
unproblematically so counted if it regularly occurs, in someone's ac-
cented speech, in all places that would normally be occupied by /I/'s.
More importantly, for many speakers, an /I/ is said quite differently when
followed by an /r/ (as in "sir") than when followed by an /L/ (as in "sill");
it is said quite differently when followed by a "front" consonant like /p/
(as in "sip") than when followed by a "back" consonant like /k/ (as in
"sick"). In fact, in my dialect, the sound /I/ is said in exactly the same
way as the vowel sound in a word like "set" (represented as /E/) when
these two vowels occur before nasal consonants, so the words *pin* and
pen are, in my dialect, said in the same way.

What makes something an /I/ is in part a matter of the entire linguistic
context. An /I/ is a complex association of various sound features
(amplitude, energy at various frequencies) out of which vowels are
composed, where the presence of these features takes on differing
degrees of significance depending on the contexts in which the vowel
occurs, such as the age of the speaker (the overall pitch of the voice) and
the surrounding consonants, as well as many other such contextual
features (among them, the stress or loudness of the word, the rate of
speaking, and so forth). Thus, even for such a simple cultural property
as a vowel, we are very quickly involved with an abstract and holistic
characterization, captured by a network of associations, and no simple
physical characterizations (such as "all /I/'s have a fundamental frequency
of value X"). What holds for phonemes like /I/ holds also for a great
many other features recognizable by humans: colors, faces, flowers,
trees, animals, voices, smells, feelings, songs, words, and, importantly,
given our discussion in the last chapter, meanings.

It is important to see what sort of power we buy when we model the
mind by a "brainlike" neuronal metaphor of the sort embodied in
connectionist networks. The brain contains a total of something like 10^{11}
neurons with an average of at least 10^3 connections each (P. M.
Churchland, 1989: 190; see also P. S. Churchland, 1986). Thus, the
human brain has something like 10^{14} total connection weights to play
with (10^{14} connections that can be weighted to different degrees,
depending upon how important the signal being sent by the sending unit
is to the operation of the receiving unit).

We have seen that learning is a matter of adjusting the values of these
weights across the whole network so as to give just the right discrimina-
tions as output (for example, rocks as rocks and mines as mines). The
brain is obviously composed of a great many separate but interconnected

networks. The total number of distinct configurations of connection weights across the brain amounts to the total number of different views of the world we can have, or "theories" about the world we can entertain (our view of cats, honor, beauty, humans, God, the differences between rocks and mines, or between men and women, and everything else in the world, discriminated by all the networks the brain can make available). If we conservatively estimate that each weight admits of only 10 possible values, the total number of distinct possible configurations of connection weights (that is, distinct possible positions in weight space), given that the brain has a total of 10^{14} connection weights to play with, is 10 for the first weight, times 10 for the second weight, times 10 for the third weight, and so on, for a total of $10^{1,014}$, or 10 raised to the power of 100 billion. This is the total number of (just barely) distinguishable theories embraceable by a human. To put this number into some perspective, we can note that the total number of elementary particles in the entire universe is only about 10^{87}. Thus, there are more overall theories of the world that the brain can entertain than there are elementary particles in the universe.

We can also meditate on the fact that at any one time a given human being holds and acts on only one of these innumerable theories. How likely is it to be the one out of all these innumerable theories that is either "correct" or conducive to a humane and good life? Certainly there is ample room, in the brain and in the world, for the consideration of alternatives. In Chapter 4, I will argue that the brain is not, in fact, searching for "true" or "humane" theories, but for "satisfying" ones, theories that make sense of a person's experience within the constraints of the sociocultural groups to which he or she belongs. Unfortunately, such theories often advantage one's self and one's groups at the expense of "truth," as well as the interests of others. That is, such theories are rootedly ideological.

THERE ARE NO SCHEMAS: ROOMS IN THE MIND AND THE WORLD

I want now to turn to a slightly different example of a network. This network is, in principle, pretty much the same as the mine/rock network, but we will make somewhat different use of it. It was developed for use as an example in McClelland, Rumelhart, and Hinton (1986). In addition to McClelland, Rumelhart, and Hinton's work, my discussion in this section is greatly influenced by Andy Clark's excellent book,

Microcognition: Philosophy, Cognitive Science, and Parallel Distributed Processing (1989).

Let us imagine two New York street gangs, the Jets and Sharks. Some of the facts about them are presented in Table 2.1.

One way to encode and store information of the kind listed in Table 2.1 is with a network, which may be represented as in Figure 2.3. In Figure 2.3, the following conventions are adopted:

1. Irregular clouds signify the existence of mutual inhibitory links among all the units within a cloud. Thus, consider the cloud in Figure 2.3 with the three units "20's," "30's," and "40's" inside it. This cloud has three units in it, one signifying that the individual concerned is in his twenties, another signifying that an individual is in his thirties, and so on. Since no one can be both in his twenties and in his thirties or forties, the units are set up to be mutually inhibitory. To keep Figure 2.3 from being yet more cluttered, I have not drawn connections between each of the units in this (or the other) clouds, but each unit is connected to the others with a link that is inhibitory, so that if the unit "20's," for instance, fires, it sends signals to the units "30's" and "40's," telling them not to fire.

2. Lines with arrowheads represent excitatory links. If the line has an arrow at each end, the link is mutually excitatory. Thus, suppose all burglars are in their thirties. There would be an excitatory link between each unit representing a burglar (that is, each solid dot connected to the burglar unit) and the 30's unit. If, in addition, *only* burglars are in their thirties, the 30's unit would be excitatorily linked to the units representing burglars.

3. The solid black spots in the middle of the figure, which I have numbered for ease of reference later, signify individual human beings. They are connected by mutually excitatory links to the properties that the individual has; for example, one such solid dot unit is linked to units representing "Lance" (a name), twenties, burglar, single, Jet, and junior-high-school education. Thus, if, for example, the unit "Lance" (the name), or the unit "single," is excited, that unit will send a certain dose of excitement to any and all solid dots connected to "Lance" and "single" (and vice versa); if both "Lance" and "single" are excited, any solid dot connected to both gets, of course, two doses of stimulation.

The network in Figure 2.3 can be viewed just like the rock/mine network discussed above. In this case, any of the units within an irregular cloud (except the solid dot units)—for example, the names Lance, Art, Rick, and so forth—could be viewed as the output we get when we feed

Table 2.1
The Jets and the Sharks

Name	Gang	Age	Education	Martial Status	Occupation
Art	Jets	40s	J.H.	single	pusher
Al	Jets	30s	J.H.	married	burglar
Sam	Jets	20s	College	single	bookie
Clyde	Jets	40s	J.H.	single	bookie
Mike	Jets	30s	J.H.	single	bookie
Jim	Jets	20s	J.H.	divorced	burglar
Greg	Jets	20s	H.S.	married	pusher
John	Jets	20s	J.H.	married	burglar
Doug	Jets	30s	H.S.	single	bookie
Lance	Jets	20s	J.H.	married	burglar
George	Jets	20s	J.H.	divorced	bookie
Pete	Jets	20s	H.S.	single	bookie
Fred	Jets	20s	H.S.	single	pusher
Gene	Jets	20s	College	single	pusher
Ralph	Jets	30s	J.H.	single	pusher
Phil	Sharks	30s	College	married	pusher
Ike	Sharks	30s	J.H.	single	bookie
Nick	Sharks	30s	H.S.	single	pusher
Don	Sharks	30s	College	married	burglar
Ned	Sharks	30s	College	married	bookie
Karl	Sharks	40s	H.S.	married	bookie
Ken	Sharks	20s	H.S.	single	burglar
Earl	Sharks	40s	H.S.	married	burglar
Rick	Sharks	30s	H.S.	divorced	burglar
Ol	Sharks	30s	College	married	pusher
Neal	Sharks	30s	H.S.	single	bookie
Dave	Sharks	30s	H.S.	divorced	pusher

Source: J. McClelland, D. Rumelhart, and G. Hinton, "The Appeal of PDP," in D. Rumelhart, J. McClelland, and the PDP Reserch Group, *Parallel Distributed Processing: Explorations in the Microstructure of Cognition*, Vol. I (Cambridge, Mass.: MIT Press, 1986), p. 27, fig. 10.

the network such features as "in his twenties, burglar, single, educated to junior-high-school level, and a Jet" as input. The solid dot units in the middle of the figure function as the hidden layer (organizing generalizations about these input features and relating them to outputs, in this case, names like Lance, which, by the way, names a single burglar in his twenties belonging to the Jets and educated to a junior-high-school level).

However, this network can also be used in somewhat different ways for somewhat different purposes. It captures the fact that certain clusters of features go together. Activating a single feature or several of them in a cluster activates in turn all the others. Consider the information that the network encodes about Rick. Rick is named "Rick," is a Shark, is in his thirties, is a burglar, is divorced, and is high-school educated. All these features cluster together and activating one or several of them will activate the rest of them.

Figure 2.3
A Network: Some of the Units and Connections Needed to Represent the Individuals Shown in Table 2.1

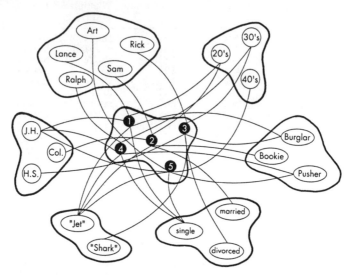

Source: Adapted from J. McClelland, D. Rumelhart, and G. Hinton, "The Appeal of PDP," in D. Rumelhart, J. McClelland, and the PDP Research Group, *Parallel Distributed Processing: Explorations in the Microstructure of Cognition*, Vol. I (Cambridge, Mass., MIT Press, 1986), p. 28, fig. 11.

It is easy to see how this works. Suppose you activate the features "is a Shark, is in his thirties." These units then pass positive values to the units represented by solid dots in the center of the figure to which they are connected by excitatory links. The unit "Shark" activates the solid dot at the upper right of the cloud containing the solid dots, the one labeled "3"; the unit "30's" activates two of the solid dots, the same one in the upper right (3) that the unit "Shark" activated, and the one on the lower left, the one labeled "4." Since two units ("Shark," "30's") are activating the dot labeled 3, it gets two "doses" of activation. The dot on the lower left, 4, is activated only by the unit "30's" and so gets only one dose of activation. Therefore (assuming the weights are all about equal), dot 3 passes greater activation along the system (yells louder). This dot, in turn, signals to (activates) the various units (features) to which it is connected in the irregular clouds surrounding the solid dot cloud. The result is a pattern of activation involving the following units: "Shark" and "30's" (both activated when we started up the system by giving it the information "Shark" and "thirties"), as well as "burglar," "divorced," a "high-school education," and (the name) "Rick," all of which are connected to the solid dot 3 that has been strongly activated by the units "Shark" and "30's."

The same final pattern of activation (that is, the overall pattern of units active after the spread of activation) could have been achieved by giving the system any one of a number of partial descriptions, for example, the inputs "Shark, high-school education," "Rick, thirties," and so on. The cluster of features that represent the person Rick "hang together," and we get all of them activated by activating any part of them.

Another interesting property of our gang network is that it is capable of behaving sensibly on the basis of data that are partial or include errors. To see this, suppose we want to retrieve the name of an individual whom we believe to be a Jet, a bookie, and educated at the junior-high-school level. In fact, no one in our model satisfies that description. The best fit is Sam, who is a bookie, a Jet, and married, but he has a college education. The network can cope thanks to the *inhibitory* links.

The system works like this. The units for "bookie," "married," "Jet," and (the mistake) a junior-high-school education are activated. The units for "bookie" and "married" directly excite only one of the solid dot units that specify individuals, namely the one I have labeled 2. The "Jet" unit excites the solid dots labeled 1, 2, 4, and 5 (only Rick, whose individual-signifying unit is labeled 3, is a Shark). The junior-high-school education unit excites solid dots 1, 4, and 5.

Thus, the solid dot 2 is stimulated three times, and solid dots 1, 4, and 5 twice (3 doesn't get any excitation, since it is connected to none of "Jet," "bookie," or "junior-high-school education"). But the various individual-representing units are themselves connected in a mutually inhibitory fashion, so the strong, threefold activation of the solid dot 2 unit will tend to inhibit the weaker, twofold activation of the 1, 4, and 5 solid dot units. And when the activation spreads outward from the solid dot units representing individuals, 2 will pass on the most significant excitatory value. This solid dot unit (2) is excitatorily linked to the name unit "Sam." And the various name units, too, are competitively connected via mutually inhibitory links. Thus, "Sam" will turn out to be the network's chosen completion of the error-involving description beginning "Jet," "bookie," "married," "junior-high-school education," which is a reasonable choice.

Finally, the system is capable of making flexible generalizations. In this case the network is used to generate a typical set of properties associated with some description, even though all the system directly knows about are individuals, none of whom needs to be a perfectly typical instantiation of the description in question. Thus, suppose we seek a sketch of the typical Jet. It turns out that there are patterns in Jet membership, although no individual Jet is a perfect example of all these patterns at once. Thus, three of the four Jets are single; three of the four are educated only to the junior-high-school level; two of the four Jets are in their twenties (one other is in his thirties, the other in his forties); and two are pushers (one other is a burglar, the other a bookie).

If the system is given "Jet" as input, the units for "single" and "junior-high-school education" will show significant activity, with three doses of activity, and each will dampen (through inhibition) the other members of its cloud, even if one of its fellow units does get a dose of activation from the fourth Jet. The units "burglar" and "30's" get two doses (so are somewhat more weakly activated than the units "single" and "junior-high-school-educated"); however, their two doses will dampen the single dose each their cloudmates get.

In this way, the network effectively generalizes to the nature of the typical Jet, that is, someone who is single and junior-high-school educated, and, with a little less surety, a burglar and in his twenties. No Jet actually meets this description; nonetheless the network can give it. And note that nowhere does the network actually store this generalization as a separate piece of information—all it contains is information about actual individuals and their properties.

This last issue, of flexible generalizations, is quite important, since it brings us to a consideration of "schemas." "Schemas" have played a major role in modern cognitive psychology (Bobrow & Collins, 1975; Mandler, 1984). Schemas (also called "scripts" or "schemata") are claimed to be special data structures in the mind that encode the stereotypical items or events associated with some description. For example, Schank and Abelson's (1977) restaurant script held data on the course of events involved in a typical visit to a restaurant. The motivation for introducing scripts and schemata was simple. Human reasoning involves filling in numerous default values in order to understand what we see or are told.

But the schema-based approach is beset by difficulties. Individual scripts or schemata prove too structured and inflexible to be able to cope with all the variants of a situation (two examples are novel situations and mixtures of stereotypic scenarios; others will readily suggest themselves) yet humans are sensible enough to take such variants in stride. The obvious way of overcoming this problem is to accept a massive proliferation of schemata; but the computational expense is prohibitive. The malleability required involves a system able to adjust the "default values" of each item in a scenario in a way that is sensitive to all the data known in the current situation. Thus, it might be reasonable to assign "some meat" as a default value for the slot "contents of refrigerator." But if you are told that the refrigerator belongs to a vegetarian, this default assignment should change. This kind of flexibility has to be explicitly provided for in any conventional schema-based approach at a cost of significant information-processing complexity.

The connectionist model using networks gets around these difficulties in a natural and unforced way by not having explicit schemas represented at all. A network contains no representational object that is a schema. Rather, schemas emerge at the moment they are needed from the interaction of the units in the network all working in concert with one another. The key to the network's ability to "mimic" schemas, without having to actually store them, is the notion of subpatterns of units that tend to come on together, because of excitatory links. The tendency can be overwhelmed by sufficient excitation and inhibition from elsewhere. But insofar as it exists, it acts like a stored schema.

Yet there is no need to decide in advance on a particular set of schemas to store. Instead, the network learns (or is told) patterns of co-occurrence of individual items making up the schema (such as the pattern of co-occurrence we saw in the case of Jets in the gang network, namely, that the units for being a Jet, being single, and being junior-high-school educated, in particular, tend to come on—get excited—together), and the rest comes in the back door when required.

The particular model detailed by McClelland, Rumelhart, and the PDP Research Group (1986, 2: 20–38; see also Clark, 1989, 92—102) concerns our understanding of a typical room, for example, a typical kitchen or a typical office. The general interest of the model is that it shows how a high-level symbolic characterization (such as, in this case, our idea of a typical kitchen, which traditional approaches would handle by saying that we had a schema for kitchens stored in our heads) can be among the "emergent properties" of a network of simpler entities. The network contains information about actual rooms and their furnishings and nowhere explicitly stores a description of a "typical kitchen," yet, we will see, the network can yield information (predictions) about a typical kitchen.

All of us have been exposed to the contents of lots of rooms. We saw objects clustering on these occasions. Generally, when you were in a room with an oven, you were in a room with a sink and not in a room with a bed. So suppose you had something like a set of our artificial neuronal units (using your real neurons, of course) responding to the presence of particular household items (this is clearly an oversimplification, since we are actually responding to features of these items in order to recognize them as a sink or a bed, but it will do for current purposes). And you fixed it so that units that tended to be on together got linked by an excitatory connection and units that tended to go on and off independently got linked by an inhibitory connection. You would get to the point where activating the unit for one prominent kitchen feature (for example the oven) would activate in a kind of chain all and only the units standing for items commonly found in kitchens. Here, then, we have an emergent schema in its grossest form. Turn on the oven unit and after a while you get (in the particular simulation done by McClelland, Rumelhart, and the PDP Research Group): oven, ceiling, walls, window, telephone, clock, coffee cup, curtains, sink, refrigerator, toaster, cupboard, and coffeepot.

The most interesting property of the room network for our current purposes is the multiplicity and flexibility of the emergent schemas it supports. McClelland, Rumelhart, and the PDP Research Group ran a simulation involving forty names of household features. After fixing connectivity weights according to a rough survey of human opinions, they found that the network "stored" five basic patterns in the sense that if you set just *one* description unit on (for example, the oven or bed unit), the system would always settle on one of five patterns of activation. But the system proved much more flexible than this state of affairs initially suggests. Many other final patterns of activation proved possible if more than one description was turned on. It will thus find a "sensible" pattern completion (subject to how sensible its stored knowledge is) even for the input pattern "bed, bath, refrigerator."

To show this in action, McClelland, Rumelhart, and the PDP Research Group describe a case where "bed, sofa" is given as the input pattern. The system then sets about trying to find a pattern of activation for the rest of its units that respects, as far as possible, all the various constraints associated with the presence of a bed and sofa simultaneously (all the other units they each tend to excite). What we want is a set of values that allows the final active schema to be sensitive to the effects of the presence of a sofa on our idea of a typical bedroom. In effect, we are asking for an unanticipated schema: a typical bedroom-with-a-sofa-in-it.

In this situation, the room network ends up choosing "large" as the size description (whereas in its basic bedroom scenario the size is set at "medium") and adding "easy chair," "floor lamp," and "fireplace" to the basic bedroom pattern (which includes television, drapes, floor lamp, picture, clock, books, carpet, bookshelf, window, door, walls, ceiling, in addition to a bed). It has added a subpattern strongly associated with "sofa," to its bedroom schema and has adjusted the size of the room accordingly. Emergent schemata obviate the need to decide *in advance* which possible situations the system will need to cope with, and they allow it to adjust its default values in a way maximally consistent with the range of possible inputs.

All networks have a property that we have not yet stressed, though it has been apparent throughout. That is, networks represent things— mines, rooms, or gang members, or whatever—as *associations distributed* over a variety of units that represent *features* of these things. The room network, for instance, represents the concept "kitchen," not by a picture of a kitchen or a general description or schema of a typical kitchen, but rather as a set of associations distributed over many units that stand for (or respond to) features of kitchens, things like sinks, coffeepots, and beds. These items themselves can be represented in networks as patterns of associations distributed over many units that stand for (or respond to) yet more basic and simpler subfeatures, features not necessarily used in our everyday talk at all, whether these be geometrical (lines, angles, textures, and so on) or functional (useful for sitting on, useful for lying down on, and so forth) properties of objects.

IMPLICATIONS OF THE GANG AND ROOM NETWORKS

The gang and the room networks are arguably good models of the sort of thing that is in our minds when we think and talk about gang members or rooms. Or when we think and talk about many other things, such as democracy, love, beauty, honor, urban violence, furniture, art forms, games, and, indeed, natural kinds like cats and rocks when we are using them in our everyday lives and no problems necessitating an appeal to internal structures arise. Like our rock/mine network, these networks hold several important implications for how we view meaning and the mind.

The moral of the network model is that what we have in our minds when we think and talk about most things—for instance, gang members— is a complex configuration of associations among a number of features which are themselves complex configurations of associations of subfeatures and so on down to possibly arbitrary configurations of neuronal patterns. These complex associative configurations need not be "obvious," "elegant," "rational," or "simple." They simply have to have been learned.

These networks of associations are certainly not open to a great amount of conscious awareness. The complex configuration of associative links that constitutes my concept (network) about gang members or games, for instance, has been formed from a huge number of concrete experiences I have had with gangs or games in my reading, talking with others, viewing television and movies, and seeing persons, objects, and events in the world. I have no idea of exactly which features are present in my network, what associations there are among them, or how they are weighted.

For example, exactly how important is wearing a certain type of cap (say, a black Oakland Raider's cap) or a certain color (red, blue), in relation to a myriad of other features, to my decision as to whether some Los Angeles teenager is a gang member? My network assigns these features each a weight and uses them in relation to all the network's other features (units) to think and talk about gangs. But my conscious awareness is certainly not privy to these massively parallel and quick workings of my mind.

Just as in the case of the mine/rock network, my mental network for gang members has a certain number of units in it at several layers, each with certain synaptic connections with weights to be set. If my gang network is as complicated as the rock/mine network (which is not all that complicated as networks go), then it has literally billions of distinct possible configurations of connection weights across the whole network (that is, a given setting of each weight in relation to all the others in the network). Each of these billions of overall weight configurations is one possible view, or *theory*, about gang members, each with its indefinitely many emergent schemas (generalizations). While I entertain one of these billions of theories at any particular time, the one I entertain seems quite unlikely to be the "best" one out of the billions of possible viewpoints or theories made possible by the nature of my mind/brain, in any sense of "best" ("correct," "useful," "humane," or whatever).

Furthermore, living in Los Angeles as I do, I am constantly having new experiences relevant to gangs, and so my network is ever changing, both in its number of units (features in terms of which gang membership can be composed), their connections (associations), and the weights (importance) of those connections. I am continually—with no necessary conscious awareness—shifting through and changing among the billions of possible theories about gang members that my network makes possible. And, remember, we are not going to run out of neurons or connections or weight spaces—we have more possible weight configurations across the brain than there are elementary particles in the universe.

Given the complexity of networks, the billions of alternative theories they make available, and their ever-changing nature, it is quite unlikely that any two people, even two people from the same "speech community," ever have identical networks in regard to such things as gangs, love, games, and democracy. Of course, these different networks may still give similar decisions ("yes," this is a gang member, game, instance of love, or "no," it's not) across a wide array of cases, as could two different weight configurations of the mine/rock network. Nonetheless, when different people's networks are integrated with other networks (and our concepts are surely hooked up in massively complex interrelationships), differences could appear at any point (we agree on who is and who isn't a gang member, but differences turn up nonetheless when we are talking about democracy within gangs). Different weight configurations are different theories.

Since my mental network for gang members is not open to my conscious awareness, is ever changing, almost certainly "wrong" at any time (though, perhaps, but just perhaps, improving), and is probably not all that similar in its details to the networks in other people's heads, it is a very poor candidate for being the meaning of the term "gang member." The same argument applies to almost any other concept—surely any complicated one like "love," "games," "education," "democracy," "freedom," "value," and so on through thousands of concepts. But networks, we are arguing, just *are* what is in our heads. So, once again, since networks are what's in our heads, and they are poor candidates for meaning, meaning isn't in our heads—we reach the same conclusion we reached in Chapter 1.

The key issue, given the complexity and variety of networks turns out to be: *How does one learn* the weight configuration for any of one's networks? After all, any reasonable network has millions or billions of possible weight configurations across its synaptic connections. How do we learn to select one of these configurations? We humans surely have no nice mathematical learning rule that some experimenter feeds into us to nudge weight configurations nearer and nearer to giving "correct" outputs, like "rock" or "mine" (Norman, 1986). We have to set up the connections between our units and the weights of those connections based on our experiences in the world.

If the weight configurations of our networks (say, our network about gang members) are to be similar enough—at least in the outputs they give—to those of other people with whom we interact, it will be crucial that we not only have a large number of experiences in common with them but that we focus on many of the same features or aspects of these experiences as the relevant ones for setting up units, connections, and weights. Since the internal workings of networks are not open to conscious awareness, others cannot just tell us what to focus on—they rarely know what they are focusing on (and even when they have overt views about the matter, they are often wrong).

The only way to ensure that learners have the right experiences and focus on the relevant aspects of them is to *apprentice* them to the *social practices* of sociocultural groups (Gee, 1990c) in such a way as to ensure that they have certain experiences and have their attention focused in the right ways through interaction with "masters" acting out their mastery. Thus, a *social community* (large or small) provides experiences and focuses the attention through carrying out its social practices and apprenticing newcomers to it.

The new art aficionado listens to an adept viewer exclaim, "See how the purple of that table gives it solidity and makes it jut out in such a way that the geometrical relations of the piece are stressed, despite its realistic portrayal of a still life," and learns *a way* of focusing on Cézanne's paintings (Gee, 1989b; Chapter 5, this book), setting "weights" across many connections of a huge number of features constituting the perception of visual objects and paintings. The middle-class mother asks for the hundredth time of a picture in a book she and her child have read repeatedly, "What's that?", "What's that say?", "Where did we see a donkey?", and the child is no longer tempted to answer, "You know, why are you asking me?" but picks up a whole *theory* of books and reading.

For some words (for example, "cat") the relevant social community is quite broad, indeed; but for many others (such as "gang member," "democracy," "race," "love"), the communities are smaller, though overlapping in complex ways. There is no doubt that "gang member" means something different for a Latino youth in a barrio and for a yuppie in a guarded-gate community. They are in different social communities engaging in different social practices (having different experiences, focusing on different features of those experiences, and they have undergone different apprenticeships).

Thus, I argue, social practices instill in people's heads different theories (that is, different versions of the billions of possible overall weight configurations in mental networks). Each head in a given social practice has, of course, a somewhat different theory, a somewhat different weight configuration, since no two people are identical or have identical experiences. However, the heads in a given social practice hold similar, or "converging, theories." By this I mean that, though they are all different and ever changing, the social practice serves as a "correcting device," nudging them each toward some "norm" or "target" theory, which no one individual need actually hold. If your network gets too far out of line, the social group will see to it that you have experiences that "reset" some weights so as to nudge your network closer to the "target" (or, in some cases, see to it that you have experiences that end your networks).

And, thus, we reach the main point: the meanings of terms like "gang member," "democracy," "games," "love," "good," "right," and so on through thousands of others, is not the *theory* (network with a particular setting of weight values across its synaptic connections) in your head, but the one embodied in the social practice that helped set those values in the first place and that keeps them (more or less) in line. This "theory," which is in the world, not in the head, is discoverable only by a species of ethnography. It is what I called a "cultural model" (Holland & Quinn, 1987) in Chapter 1, tied to what I called in that chapter a "Discourse" (see Chapter 5 below). The study of meaning, including the study of the meaning of mental terms like "believe," "think," and "remember," is not the study of the mind or brain, but of the world and the social practices of people in it.

3

MEMORY

The mind, I argued in the last chapter, is made up of networks of associations. These networks serve as the tools for engaging in social practices. The meanings of words like "cat," "love," "democracy," and "gang member" reside, not in these tools, but in the social practices connected with these words. The first two chapters of this book have been dedicated to the thesis that meaning is not in the head, but in specific social practices connected with specific sociocultural groups. In subsequent chapters, I will discuss the character of these social practices, as well as their relationships to language, literacy, and sense making. However, in this chapter, I want to take up the issue of the relationship between the mind and things that contemporary psychology takes to be "mental entities" par excellence, things like "memory."

In everyday talk and writing we all regularly use a whole host of "mental terms" like "believe," "think," "remember," and so forth. What I said in the last chapter about meaning applies equally to these terms as well. The *meaning* of the word "memory" is not something in the head, but something embedded in social practices within which various groups of people talk, think, and act out their cultural models of mind. And, indeed, different cultures, and different social groups within our own culture, have different social practices in this regard; thus, terms like "memory" and "belief" (or their "translations" into other languages) mean different things to different sociocultural groups (Clanchy, 1979; D'Andrade, 1987; Holland & Quinn, 1987; Lakoff, 1986; Lakoff & Johnson, 1980; Ong, 1958).

But the psychologist wants to know, not what ordinary people mean by "memory," but what memory "really" is. And the psychologist assumes that what memory "really" is is what the "best" scientific theory about memory says it is. The "best" theory is the one judged as "best" in terms of what counts as a "good" theory in the sciences concerned with the mind, for example, neuropsychology and cognitive psychology.

This situation is quite analogous to that of biologists attempting to specify what cats are (or viruses, to take a more realistic example that has caused a good deal of excitement in biology over the last few decades). Biologists don't care what everyday folk think about cats; rather they care about a theory of the *genetic structure and evolutionary history* of cats, a theory that makes correct predictions, relates to general knowledge about genetics and evolution, and explains phenomena biologists take it as their job to explain (by their standards of explanation).

There is an important relationship, however, between scientific theories about things like cats and ordinary, everyday folk theories or cultural models about cats (based on appearances and not structure). A scientific theory of cats must end up picking out *as cats* (in the biologist's sense) some significant number of what the folk theory picks out *as typical cats or typical types of cats* (in the everyday sense). Scientific theories about cats "reduce" (translate) everyday folk theories about cats into their own scientific language (P. S. Churchland, 1986). But the scientific theory doesn't count as a reduction of the folk theory unless there is significant overlap in what the scientist's "cat" picks out and what the folk's "cat" picks out. Otherwise, we would have no way of knowing that the scientific theory was a reduction of the folk theory of cats and not something else.

Philosophers can and will argue what sort of (and how much of an) overlap between the scientist's "cat" and the folk's "cat" counts as "significant." However, it is clear that if biologists told us that cats (in *their* theory) are the set of all foxes; my pet cat, Wicked; and a couple of opossums, this set so little overlaps with the animals taken to be typical cats by the ordinary folk that we would not say that the biological theory was a theory of cats (that it reduced the folk theory of cats). On the other hand, if biologists told us that cats are the set of all folk cats minus Maine Coon Cats, which it turns out (let us say) are more closely related (in genetic or evolutionary terms) to foxes than they are to other folk cats, then we will readily concede that they have reduced ("corrected," in the opinion, at least, of the scientist) the folk theory of cats.

The same is true of memory. "Memory," in the psychologist's sense (for example, Bartlett, 1932; Norman, 1969, 1988; Neisser, 1982), need not turn out to be what folk theories of memory say it is. But it does have to pick out as memory at least some of the central examples of memory in the folk sense. Otherwise, the psychologist's theory would be a reduction of some other folk concept than memory, or it would be a theory about some entity that folk theories don't deal with.

In this chapter, I want to argue that any theory that reduces the folk theory of memory—that is, any "scientific" view about what memory "really" is—will be a theory not primarily about what is in the mind/brain, but a theory of how the mind/brain is put to use—as a tool—within social practices. The upshot of this claim is that memory must be studied and theorized by studying social practices, not just by studying the mind/brain. An analogous argument could be made about things like believing, thinking, knowing, and so forth.

MEMORY: WHAT IS IN THE MIND/BRAIN? WHAT IS NOT?

A standard traditional view in philosophy and psychology is that memories are either images (pictures or things like films) in the mind or that they are languagelike descriptions in the mind (Neisser & Winograd, 1988). When I remember that "Nixon visited China," what I have in mind, it is claimed, is either a languagelike mental representation of the proposition named by the sentence "Nixon visited China" or some sort of image or images of Nixon, China, and Nixon visiting China.

Important current work in philosophy (P. S. Churchland, 1986; P. M. Churchland, 1989; Johnson, 1991; McClelland, Rumelhart, & the PDP Research Group, 1986; Rumelhart, McClelland, the PDP Research Group, 1986) is beginning to seriously challenge this view of memory and related notions like believing and thinking. This new work claims that memory is a *connectionist network* in the mind, of the sort we looked at in the last chapter, or, rather, a large set of such networks. However, I will argue that these networks *are not* themselves memories (or beliefs), but rather tools by which we play memory (and belief) "games," that is, engage in social practices of certain sorts.

The argument that memory is not something in individual heads, but something fully caught up with and residing in social practices will take us a while to develop (for an interesting discussion of how psychology forgot that memory is a social practice, see Shotter, 1990). The upshot will be to render the mind/brain not all that relevant to the study of memory (though not completely irrelevant). I will develop my view of memory through the use of the little scenario below (Gee, 1989a).

Imagine, for the time being, that this scenario describes some events that happened in the "real" world:

The Alligator River Episode

1. There was a woman named Abigail.
2. She was in love with a man named Gregory.
3. Gregory lived on island in the middle of a river.
4. Abigail lived on the mainland across from the island.
5. The river that separated the two lovers was teeming with people-eating alligators.
6. Abigail wanted to cross the river to visit Gregory.
7. Unfortunately, the bridge had been washed out.
8. So she went to ask Jerome, a riverboat captain, to take her across.
9. He said he would be glad to take her across, if she would consent to go to bed with him preceding the voyage.
10. She promptly refused and went to a friend named Ivan to explain her plight.
11. Ivan did not want to be involved in the situation.
12. Abigail felt her only alternative was to accept Jerome's terms.
13. Jerome fulfilled his promise to Abigail and delivered her into the arms of Gregory.
14. When she told Gregory about her sexual submission in order to cross the river, Gregory cast her aside with disdain.
15. Heartsick and dejected, Abigail asked her friend Sid to punish Gregory.
16. Sid, feeling compassion for Abigail, sought out Gregory and beat him up.
17. Abigail was overjoyed at the sight of Gregory getting his due.
18. Abigail laughed at Gregory when she heard the news that he had been beaten up.

Imagine someone, let us call her Kris, was privy to these events—through witnessing them or hearing about them or some combination of the two. Let us say, then, that Kris has experienced and now remembers a certain *episode*, namely the episode captured by sentences 1–18, in "the above alligator river episode." Having experienced the events of this episode, Kris also remembers a number of what I will call "dated particulars," that is, individual events or states like "At time t [whatever time it happened to be], Jerome propositioned Abigail" or "During a certain span of time t_i–t_j (whatever it happened to be), Abigail loved Gregory."

Let us imagine that the contents of this alligator river episode are stored in Kris's mind/brain as a *network of associations* among all the people and events she has experienced and their various properties. Of course, Kris has experienced many more people and events than those in 1–18 above. Her network of associations among people, events, and their properties is, undoubtedly, massive and multidimensional. But then, as we saw in the last chapter, there are billions of neurons and neural connections in the brain. It would be impossible to draw any fair representation of Kris's network in two dimensions on a piece of paper. However, consider Table 3.1, which lists just a small number of the associations such a network (in Kris's head) encodes:

Table 3.1 simply lists certain relationships. I represent time as an arbitrary set of numbers such that time t_8 is after time t_7 and before time t_9, and the time span running from time t_{10} to time t_{50} lies within the time span running from time t_5 to time t_{110}. I have no idea how the mind/brain represents time. An *agent* is an initiator of an action, while an *experiencer* is one who experiences a state, like love or death. A *patient* is one who undergoes the effects of some action or state, like being beaten or being loved (on terms like "agent" and "patient," see Jackendoff, 1983, 1990). The table says that during the time span running from time t_{45} to time t_{50} there is a set of associations among the island, Abigail, Gregory, and the act of visiting such that Abigail is an agent (the one who initiates the visit), Gregory is a patient (the one who gets visited), and the island is a Location (a place where the visiting took place).

Each of the "units" in the first row of the table will be associated with many other units. Other things happened during the time span t_{45}–t_{50}, Abigail is associated with many other people and acts, and so are Gregory and the island. Imagine, then, that each of these (moments and spans of time, the island, Abigail, Gregory, and visiting) is just a unit in a large network, with many links to many other such units (other times, other people, other acts and states).

Table 3.1 also shows that Abigail loved Gregory during a subset of the time span in which Susan loved Gregory and that during that same time span (in which Susan loved Gregory) Jerome loved Susan. Other acts and states are captured in an obvious way. Of course, there will also be links between the various actions and states. If in Kris's experience a good many lovers have ended up visiting or trying to visit their loved

Table 3.1
Some Relationships from Kris's Mental Network in Regard to the Alligator River Events

TIME	LOCATION	AGENT/ EXPERI- ENCER	PATIENT	ACT/STATE
$t_{45} - t_{50}$	Island	Abigail	Gregory	Visit
$t_2 - t_{100}$		Susan	Gregory	Love
$t_2 - t_{60}$		Abigail	Gregory	Love
$t_2 - t_{100}$		Jerome	Susan	Love
t_{65}	Mainland	Abigail	Jerome	Complains to
$t_2 - t_{65}$		Jerome	Gregory	Jealous of
t_{40}	Riverbank	Jerome	Abigail	Proposition
t_{70}	Island	Sid	Gregory	Beat up
Etc.	Etc.	Etc.	Etc.	Etc.

ones, this will create an association between loving and visiting or between loving and wanting to visit.

Another way to look at Table 3.1, when we view it as part of a large network of multiple associations, is as a set of many sub-networks. A "unit" like Jerome is linked to (associated with) a great many other units in a good many subnetworks. For instance, the unit Jerome is linked to the units t_2-t_{100}, Experiencer, Susan, Patient, and Love in one little subnetwork ("Jerome loved Susan during the time span t_2-t_{100}"), and one way in which we could link them all up is have them activate a "hidden unit" when they all get activated together. The Jerome unit is also linked to the units t_2-t_{65}, Experiencer, Gregory, Patient, and Jealous of in another configuration ("Jerome was jealous of Gregory during the time span t_2-t_{65}"); and the unit Jerome is also linked to the units t_{40}, Riverbank, Agent, Abigail, Patient, and Proposition in yet another configuration of associations ("Jerome propositioned Abigail at time t_{40}").

Each of the units in these little configurations have links to other units in other little subnetworks in a multidimensional space (for example, Love, Jealous, and Proposition are each associated with many other events Kris has experienced). When we activate the unit Jerome, it activates, in turn, many other units with which it has associations (like

Abigail, Gregory, Susan, Love, Jealous of, Proposition) and many subnetworks of these units (for example, the configuration t_{40}, River-bank, Agent Jerome, Patient Abigail, Proposition, "Jerome proposi-tioned Abgail at time t_{40} at the riverbank"). It is as if little lights go on throughout the system with varying degrees of brightness (depending upon how strongly each unit has been lit up), and in places there are clusters of lights representing little configurations. The actual im-plementation of the network could take various forms and is, in any case, beyond the scope of this book.

Now, let us take up our original question as to what memory is. What does it mean to say that Kris remembers the alligator river episode? By this, I do not mean to ask what we mean by this in our everyday folk theory of mind and memory, but what we *ought* to mean by it if we want to capture what memory "really" is, that is, what a viable scientific theory of the mind ought to say it is. The beginning of an answer to this question lies, I believe, in considering the form that any verbal report of this episode must take.

Regardless of what language this episode is reported in, it will take a certain form thanks to the way the linguistic encoding of experience works in any and every culture. Any clause[1] in such an account will name either an event in the foreground of the report or an event or state in the background of the report (Gee, 1990a; Gee, Michaels, & O'Connor, 1991; Hopper & Thompson, 1980, 1982).

In English, clauses naming foregrounded events usually have the following properties: (1) they are main clauses (not embedded in or subordinated to another clause); (2) they contain a "real" verb (not something like the copula "to be"); (3) the verb names an action (like "ran"), not a state (like "love" or the passive form "was killed"); (4) the verb is in the simple past tense (for example, *ran*, not *is/was running* or *had run*, and so forth—however, there is also a "historical present" in English, used to make reports of the past "vivid").[2] Analogous properties hold in all languages. Clauses that do not have these properties name background information.

In the sentences of the alligator river episode, sentences 1–7 all contain only background information. None of them contains a main clause with an action verb in the simple past tense. It is not until we get to sentence 8 that we get a verb naming an action in the simple past tense ("she *went* to ask Jerome . . . to take her across"). This is the start of the foregrounded events ("the plot"). Following this, we get a series of further foregrounded events (main clauses containing action verbs in the simple past): *said* . . . (9); *refused and went to* . . . (10); *fulfilled* . . .

(13); *delivered* . . . (13); *cast her aside* . . . (14); *turned to* . . . (15); *sought out and beat* . . . (16); and *laughed at* (18), interspersed with additional background information such as: *not want to be involved* . . . (11); *felt* . . . (12); *feeling compassion* . . . (16); *was overjoyed* . . . (17); and *getting* . . . (17). The foregrounded information gives the "plot" or the "main line" or the "key events." The background information gives information in terms of which the foreground can be understood or interpreted (Labov & Waletsky, 1967; Labov, 1972c).

Let us first consider the import of the foreground information in a report (imagine, for instance, that Kris had used sentences 1–18 to report the episode she remembered—my comments would hold true no matter how she had reported them). The first point I want to make is that whether some information is foregrounded or backgrounded in a report has nothing to do with how it is stored in the mind of the reporter. Whether a piece of information is foregrounded or backgrounded has to do, rather, with how one chooses to linguistically encode the information at the time of (in the context of) telling it.

For instance, Kris's mental network has a subnetwork capturing a configuration of relations having to do with Abigail visiting Gregory. Visiting is only mentioned in the report as backgrounded information ("Abigail wanted to cross the river to visit Gregory," sentence 6, where "visit," though an action, is embedded under a verb naming a mental state, *want*). However, this information could just as well (in a different telling) have appeared (been encoded) as foregrounded information, as in something like: "Wanting to be with Gregory, *Abigail visited Gregory on the island.*"

On the other hand, Kris's report treats Abigail's initial refusal of Jerome's proposition in sentence 10 as foreground ("She promptly *refused* and went to a friend named Ivan to explain her plight"), but the refusal could as well (in another telling) be treated as background as in something like: "After Abigail had refused Jerome's terms, she went to a friend named Ivan to explain her plight," where only going to Ivan (*went*) is treated as foreground. Thus, foregrounding and backgrounding are not in the mind (the mental network). Rather, they are in the ("real time," "on line") linguistic encoding of the report, and this encoding can change with the contexts in which Kris chooses to report the episode.

Linguistic encoding is a joint product of (1) Kris's mental network, (2) the linguistic system, both in terms of language universals and specific properties of English (Givon, 1979, 1989), (3) the "on line," "real time" processing (planning, problem solving, inferencing, guessing) that Kris is doing as she speaks (Levelt, 1989), (4) Kris's continually adaptive judgments about what the context is (e.g., her judgments about what her interlocutors know, expect, and are thinking, feeling, and doing, Hodge & Kress, 1988; Hodge, 1990), (5) the cues Kris is receiving from her interlocutors that signal to her how they expect her report to be structured in terms of their socioculturally based expectations (Scollon & Scollon, 1981), and (6) Kris's own socialization within various groups that report things in certain ways in certain contexts (Gee, 1990c).

Some of these things are, assuredly, in Kris's head; but some are not—for instance, the linguistic system, cues from interlocutors, contexts, and patterns of socialization are not in Kris's head, however much they may have effects on her head. And, furthermore, all of these, save item 1, are not in the mental network (or whatever else) that psychologists typically take to represent Kris's passive store of memories. All besides item 1 are active, changing, often made-up-on-the-spot mental processes or not mental processes at all, but things in the world or in other people's minds.

The second point relevant to foregrounding that I want to make is that the foregrounded part (the basic plot) of Kris's report *starts and ends* at particular places (it starts with Abigail going to Jerome in sentence 8 and ends with Abigail laughing at Gregory in sentence 18). But this too is not in the mental network, which has no markers for the beginnings and endings of what one takes to be the key events in a episode.

For instance, imagine that Kris has stored in her mental network information about Abigail's having phoned her mother, prior to deciding to visit Gregory, to ask her advice about her relationship with Gregory. Kris could have used this information either as background or foreground information (or not used it all). In particular, she could have started the foreground events in her report with something like: "Having decided she missed Gregory too much, *Abigail phoned her mother to ask her advice about what to do*" (where the underlined clause is foregrounded). Kris could thereafter have gone on to eventually get to the information encoded in the first foregrounded clause in sentences 1–18 (in sentence 8). Likewise, she could have ended with an additional foregrounded clause (perhaps with the fact that Gregory left the island for good). The report (in 1–18) as it stands ends with Abigail laughing at Gregory, and thus ends on Abigail's perspective. It could, on another telling, have ended with information about Gregory that tilted the episode more toward Gregory's perspective.

Since the first or last piece of foregrounded information in the report of an episode is a choice made in linguistically encoding the episode, the episode itself as a bounded unit with a beginning and ending is *not* in the mental network, but in the linguistic encoding, which can (and will) change with the contexts in which it is carried out. This is important enough a point to bear repeating: episodes are not in the physical happenings of the world, which are continuous, nor are they in the head, which contains as its store of information a network of diverse associations—*they are in the telling*. I do not deny that each of us has, in all likelihood, "memorized" some episodes (which are, then, in a sense, in our heads), but the vast majority of the episodes we report are "made up on the spot" in the telling. The "memorized" ones, often taken as typical by psychology, are not, in fact, anywhere near typical.

Much the same sort of things we have said about the foreground of a report can be said about the background information in the report. What is backgrounded or foregrounded, as we have just said, is not represented in the mental network of associations but is a choice made in the linguistic encoding. The background is the *interpretive framework* within which the foreground makes sense (and, thus, it is certainly not "unimportant"); it is that information against which the foreground is placed so that the foregrounded material stands out as making a certain point or having a certain significance (Gee, 1990a). Thus, too, this interpretive framework is not in the mental network, but in the contextually variable linguistic encoding of the report.

The pieces (units and subnetworks) of the mental network corresponding to the events that got placed in the foreground of a report are linked to a great many other units and subnetworks in the mental network. Any of this information could have been placed in the background of the report and thereby could have served as part of the interpretive framework. Nothing in the mental network determines what gets so placed (though, presumably, such material must be strongly activated by or associated with the pieces of the network that have gotten encoded as foregrounded information in the report, but then there is undoubtedly lots of such strongly activated information). What gets so placed is an artifact of the linguistic encoding, not the mental network.

For example, notice in Table 3.1 that both Abigail and Susan loved Gregory and that during the time both women loved Gregory, Jerome loved Susan. We can imagine an interpretive framework in which Jerome's attempting to coerce Abigail is due to his jealousy that Susan loved Gregory and not him. This interpretive framework, in fact, is not used in the telling represented in 1–18—though in all likelihood this information about Susan, Gregory, and Jerome is activated in Kris's mind by the mention of or thinking of Gregory and Abigail. It may well get mentioned in another account in another context (Tannen, 1989).

Now we reach, at last, the point of this discussion of episodes, foregrounding and backgrounding. These, as we have seen, are constructs of the linguistic encoding of the episode; they are not *in* the mental network storing Kris's experience (her so-called memory bank). All the mental network contains are associations between people, times, places, actions, and states. The "episode" as a set of foregrounded events interpreted via a set of backgrounded events and states isn't in the mind. It's in a linguistic encoding carried out at a particular time and place. Thus, what psychologists call "episodic memory" surely is not solely in the head. A viable theory of episodic memory cannot be constructed by looking only inside the head. Such a theory would have to investigate the nature of linguistic encodings in which episodes, with their characteristic foreground-background structure, arise in the first place. I will turn to the nature of this encoding—whether and how it is in the head or in the world—in a moment. First, there is one last hope to find memories in the head. We turn now to this last hope.

Someone who believes that what memory "really is" is something in the head can concede our discussion about episodic memory but still claim that the memory of a *dated particular* like *Abigail's having asked Sid to punish Gregory at a given time* is in Kris's head, whether stored as some image, some mental sentencelike entity, or as a set of associations in a (sub)network. Perhaps the way we put such dated particulars together into episodes is an artifact of encoding in context, but surely (it will claimed) the mind contains a wealth of such dated particular memories (for example, "I can just *see* Mom cutting the cake at my seventh birthday party in my head like a picture"). Alas, even this is not necessarily true.

There are two problems. First, many dated particulars need not be stored (passively) in the head, since one can infer them at the time of telling a report of an episode involving the dated particular. For example, consider sentence 15 in Kris's report of the alligator river story ("Heartsick and dejected, Abigail asked her friend Sid to punish Gregory"). It may well be that all Kris experienced, and even that all she has in her mental network, is that Abigail said to Sid: "That Gregory did me wrong. I hope he gets *his* some day." In our culture, saying such a thing can be, *in certain contexts, though not others,* taken as an indirect request for the person addressed to *do* something to Gregory (Givon, 1989; Levinson, 1983; Manktelow & Over, 1990. It can be an indirect request for punitive action, however, only if the relationship between Abigail and Sid is of the right sort.

Now Kris can assume that Sid interpreted Abigail's remark as an indirect request and go on to say that Abigail told him to punish Gregory (as Kris does in sentence 15), or she could have just said what Abigail literally said and let the hearer guess how Sid interpreted the remark. Kris's mental network need contain only the original remark. Sentence 15 represents an inference that Kris has encoded (her inference about Sid's inference), not the actual content of what is in Kris's network (which may only be what Abigail actually said).

Of course, some sentences in a report may fairly faithfully reflect dated particulars that are represented fairly directly in the mental network. Perhaps "Jerome beat Gregory up on the island at time t_{70}" is such a case; perhaps something like "Mom smiled while she cut my birthday cake on my seventh birthday" is too. But some sentences will not reflect directly what's in the mind (but inferences from what's in the mind), and *none need do so*. Thus, perhaps too, the sentence saying that Jerome beat up Gregory is an inference from knowing that Jerome hit Gregory, and Jerome is much bigger than Gregory, and Gregory considers even a small hurt a big deal. Perhaps only these latter "simpler" propositions reflect what's in Kris's mind. The point is that the report gives us no good indication of what is in the mind, even at the level of dated particulars, which seem (but really aren't) good candidates for "mental pictures" or simple propositions in the mind. Nonetheless, though "Abigail told Jerome to beat up Gregory" or even "Jerome beat up Gregory" may not be in the mind, but inferences drawn at the time of telling, they surely are part of the memory and relevant to the study of memory.

The second problem with saying that the memory of at least (some) dated particulars (like Mom cutting the cake) are in the mind is yet more important. Let us concede that someone's mental network contains a representation for a certain dated particular (perhaps a subnetwork capturing a configuration of associations that are bonded together, like Mom cutting the cake). Further, let us concede that this given dated particular is fairly straightforwardly encoded (say, "Jerome beat Gregory up on the island at time t_{70}" or "Mom cut the cake at 7:10 P.M. on October 14, 1978"). Nonetheless, this dated particular is *not a memory* unless time t_{70} or October 14, 1978, is sequenced with other dated particulars so as to give this dated particular some sense or meaning. A mind/brain could not have in it just one dated particular, because, then, the "dated particular" could not be *dated* at all, since there would be no other events to anchor it in time.

Any mental network contains thousands or millions of other events that happened before and after this one, associated with it more or less strongly. Any particular sequencing of a subset of these events that gives this dated particular any sense resides only in a choice of what else it will be foregrounded and backgrounded against, and *that* is in contextually variable encodings, not in the network, thus, not in the head. The dated particular only becomes a *memory* in such a framework. Outside this framework, it is simply a set of units firing away in a great many complex patterns depending upon what other units are firing.

Thus, even Mom cutting the birthday cake is *a memory* only to the extent that it is sequenced as part of an episode with a foreground-background structure and thus set in an interpretive framework that gives it meaning. Apart from episodes, Mom cutting the cake is part of millions of associations—it relates to nearly everything and thus "means everything," and therefore it means nothing in particular. Mom cutting the cake exists as a meaningful memory only within some episodic structure (and it can be part of indefinitely many, depending on context). Since episodes are not in the head, but in the linguistic encoding, then, in any meaningful sense, Mom's cutting the cake *as a memory* isn't either.

The therapist convinces us that Mom's resentment at not having pursued a career is connected with her somewhat feigned glee at cutting our cake. Upon hearing this, a piece of information (the somewhat forced nature of Mom's smile) that is only weakly associated in our stored mental network with the cake cutting gets into a sequence with it in such a way as to "change the story," and thus too, the meaning of the dated particular of Mom cutting the cake. Apart from such happenings—tellings, retellings, discoveries, clues from others and their tellings—the dated particular isn't a memory, just a fleeting pattern of neurons firing in the brain.

We reach a conclusion that does some violence both to folk theories of memory and to "specialist" theories in philosophy and psychology as well. Memory is "really" not in the head. Of course, there is some stuff in the head, namely networks of associations. What is in the head has the *potential* to be encoded in certain ways in certain contexts and in other ways in other contexts. What is in the head is a *tool* that we use to linguistically encode what count as memories, to play "memory games" or engage in social practices in regard to memories (see Connerton, 1989; Douglas, 1986; and Middleton & Edwards, 1990, for excellent discussion of the social nature of memory). But to count the tool as memory is as silly as to claim that hammers and saws *are* carpentry. To study the tool in order to understand memories is as silly as to study hammers and saws in order to understand buildings. You will get some way in your study, of course, since not just anything can be built with a hammer and saw, but you would get a lot further if you studied buildings and the craft that builds them.

In Chapter 1, I argued that meaning (of words and texts) is not in the head, but in the world of social practices and the cultural models they instantiate; so far in this chapter I have argued that memory and other "mental entities" (for which an analogous argument could be made) aren't in the head either. So far I have rather vaguely said that memory is in *linguistic encodings* that change with changing contexts. It is time now to unpack this jargon and see what it really amounts to. We must eventually answer the question as to where these linguistic encodings are: in the mind, the mouth, the language, or the social world?

PERSONAL MEMORY, HISTORICAL MEMORY, MYTHIC MEMORY

We imagined above that the alligator river episode was the report of someone's personal experience, meaning not that they "saw" everything, but that they "participated" in the events closely enough that we will accept their "right" to report it as a personal experience. We claimed that the memory of this episode is not "in" the head of the person who experienced it, but "in" the structuring given to the episode through its linguistic encoding. Another way to put this claim is to say that memories are not memories unless they have *plots*, and plots reside in the foreground-background structuring of "reports" (whether written, spoken, signed, or imagined).

What was said above about personal memory applies also to "historical memory." Just as many people think that memories are "in the head," they think that history is out in "in the world." But, like personal memories, history is not history unless it has a plot, and plots are not in the world apart from linguistic encoding; they are in the structure of the telling, writing, signing, or imagining. The world of "actual" people, actions, and events does not come demarcated into "beginnings" and "ends," into what count as "foregrounded," "mainline," "key" events, and what count as "background" states and events through which these foreground events make sense (are seen to be appropriately foregrounded). Rather, the historian must make such choices; "historical episodes" do not exist outside them (White, 1973).

The positioning of Russian missiles in Cuba in 1962 precipitated a "historical episode" often referred to as the "Cuban missile crisis." The stationing of American missiles as close to the Soviet Union even earlier was not defined as a crisis by either country. As Murray Edelman (1988) has said: "A crisis, like all news developments, is a creation of the language used to depict it; the appearance of a crisis is a political act, not a recognition of a fact or a rare situation" (31).

Once again, one might "buy" this argument about episodes and still attempt to claim that "historical facts" (like our dated particulars of personal experience above) are out there "in the world." But once again, something only counts as a "fact," indeed, is only recognizable at all, by being associated with other "facts" in a meaningful sequence. Just as the mind could not contain one "dated particular," because then nothing would date it, so too, history cannot contain one "fact" all by itself. We would have no idea when this "fact" occurred. But to put it in a sequence means making choices about "billions" of "happenings" that could be reported as "facts," making choices about what will count as a fact and which facts will get into the sequence and which will be foregrounded and which others backgrounded. That is to say, it means *emplotting* the world (White, 1978).

Thus, too, historical memories are epiphenomena (or, better put, "emergent properties") of episodes, and episodes are in the structure of the encoding (telling, writing, imagining), not in the world, any more than dated particulars and memories of episodes of personal experience are in the head. People who have no plots have no memories, though they would have minds/brains; people who have no plots have no history, though they would have a physical world.

There is, in fact, no sharp and clear boundary between personal memory ("my memory") and historical memory ("a society's memory"). The difference resides solely in what *social practice* one takes one's report (telling, writing, signing, imagining) to be *accountable* to. An episode about my father's being mistaken for General Dwight Eisenhower during my family's trip to Spain in the 1950s does not "announce" that it is "personal" and not "historical." If I report it as a personal memory, I take it to be an episode in my personal biography and accept the responsibility that it makes sense within this larger plot (Freccero, 1986). The nature of this responsibility varies with the sociocultural group within which I contract the responsibility. Different groups view life histories differently, and, thus, tell them and think about them in different terms.

This episode can only be reported as a piece of history, by myself or someone else, if the reporter (1) takes it to be an episode in the "historical" biography of a socioculturally defined group of people and (2) accepts the responsibility that it make sense within this larger plot. The nature of this responsibility varies either with what a group of people takes history and historical accounts to be ("folk theories of history") or with what the "science" of history (at different times and within different theories) takes history and historical facts and historical accounts to be.

Many cultures have made a distinction between "historical" time and memory, "personal" time and memory, and a third category, namely, "mythical" time and memory (Campbell, 1990; Hymes, 1981; Leach, 1969, 1976; Lévi-Strauss, 1963, 1964–1971, 1966, 1979). Episodes in mythical memory are taken to have happened in a "special" ("sacred") time ("before history") and, often, in a "special" place. The teller of mythic stories takes them to be part of the "spiritual" biography of a group of people and accepts the responsibility that the story make sense within this larger framework. This responsibility varies, of course, with the cultural tradition and mythic system of the people whose mythic story it is.

People often mistakenly make a distinction between history as "true" and "myths" as false. But to any group with an active system of mythology this is a "category" mistake—mythic events happened in a different time and place, a different dimension of "reality," in fact, from either personal or historical events. Thus, they are simply not in competition with historical events for some honorific label like "true." It is also sometimes said that cultures with mythological systems don't know what history is. This is also a mistake. They may not have anything like history as a profession (and they may), and they often don't, of course, have written history (because they don't have writing at all, at least not academic writing). But they can most certainly tell whether a "fact" is part of the story of themselves as individuals, or of the story of their group in nonmythic time, or part of the story of their group in mythic time.

Finally, it is also a mistake to believe that mythological stories are simply memorized and constitute an unchanging and finite body of stories. The teller of a mythic story accepts that his or her account must make sense within the framework of a *system* of mythology, a system that sets (in large, but total part) the structure of individual stories and allows for the generation of new ones (Propp, 1968). It is a generative system, and new stories can and do occur (we will see how below).

The distinctions between "personal memory," "historical memory," and "mythic memory" are a matter of *degree* and reside in the ways episodes are encoded in the telling or the imagining, as well as in the responsibilities the encoder takes him- or herself to have contracted. A mythic story can come to be shaped as a historical one, as a historical one can come to be shaped as mythical. And I can tell my personal story in ways that are influenced by mythic stories, as I can come to shape my personal biography as part of an historical narrative. Once again, the details reported in the episodes do not wear "tags" proclaiming that they are personal memories, historical ones, or mythic elements. The episodic structuring of these details and the larger frame to which they are held accountable settles the matter, but often with plenty of room for ambiguity and dispute. In fact, individuals and groups often fight over (and want to fight over) whether something is personal, historical, or mythical ("spiritually important").

MYTH

In the previous section, I argued that personal, historical, or mythic accounts differ only in what sort of larger "story" ("biography") the reporter takes the account to be part of and what sort of social practice the reporter assumes responsibility toward. I believe that we can come to understand the nature of memory in a deeper way if we work "backward" from "mythic memory" to "historical memory" and thence to "personal memory."

In premodern societies mythic stories constituted a socially shared "reservoir of meanings and structures of thought" (Connerton, 1989, 56–57), from which people could draw to create new meanings that resembled, echoed, cohered with older ones. The symbolic content of myth (symbols of "deeper" meanings germane to the "spiritual" nature of human beings and human existence) is not exhausted in any single formal arrangement of its characters and events. Rather, the mythic system offers many potential arrangements of the same sorts of characters and events, each of which count as a solution to a particular problem within the culture or within human existence more generally.

To see what I am talking about here, let us consider two stories from the Old Testament. One is the famous Abraham and Isaac story, the other is a somewhat less well known "variant" of the Abraham and Isaac story, or, in other words, an alternate arrangement of the same sorts of characters and events—the story of Jephthah and his daughter (The following translations are from *The New Oxford Annotated Bible*, Oxford: Oxford University Press, 1973):

Abraham and Isaac

1. After these things God tested Abraham, and said to him, "Abraham!" And he said, "Here am I."

2. He said, "Take your son, your only son Isaac, whom you love, and go to the land of Mori'ah, and offer him there as a burnt offering upon one of the mountains of which I shall tell you."

3. So Abraham rose early in the morning, saddled his ass, and took two of his young men with him, and his son Isaac; and he cut the wood for the burnt offering, and arose and went to the place of which God had told him.

4. On the third day Abraham lifted up his eyes and saw the place afar off.

5. Then Abraham said to his young men, "Stay here with the ass; I and the lad will go yonder and worship, and come again to you."

6. And Abraham took the wood of the burnt offering, and laid it on Isaac his son; and he took in his hand the fire and the knife. So they went both of them together.

7. And Isaac said to his father Abraham, "My father!" And he said, "Here am I, my son." He said, "Behold, the fire and the wood, but where is the lamb for burnt offering?"

8. Abraham said, "God will provide himself the lamb for a burnt offering, my son." So they went both of them together.

9. When they came to the place of which God had told him, Abraham built an altar there, and laid the wood in order, and bound Isaac his son, and laid him on the altar, upon the wood.

10. Then Abraham put forth his hand, and took the knife to slay his son.

11. But the angel of the Lord called to him from heaven, and said, "Abraham, Abraham!" And he said, "Here I am."

12. He said, "Do not lay your hand on the lad or do anything to him; for now I know that you fear God, seeing you have not withheld your son, your only son from me."

13. And Abraham lifted up his eyes and looked, and behold, behind him was a ram, caught in a thicket by his horns; and Abraham went and took the ram, and offered it up as a burnt offering instead of his son.

14. So Abraham called the name of that place The Lord will provide; as it is said to this day, "On the mount of the Lord it shall be provided."

15. And the angel of the Lord called to Abraham a second time from heaven,

16. and said, "By myself I have sworn, says the Lord, because you have done this, and have not withheld your son, your only son,

17. I will indeed bless you, and I will multiply your descendants as the stars of heaven and as the sand which is on the seashore. And your descendants shall possess the gate of their enemies,

18. and by your descendants shall all the nations of the earth bless themselves, because you have obeyed my voice."

19. So Abraham returned to his young men, and they arose and went together to Beersheba; and Abraham dwelt at Beersheba. (Genesis 22:1–19)

Jephthah and His Daughter

29. Then the Spirit of the Lord came upon Jephthah, and he passed through Gilead and Manas'seh, and passed on to Mizpah of Gilead, and from Mizpah of Gilead he passed on the Ammonites.

30. And Jephthah made a vow to the Lord, and said, "If thou wilt give the Ammonites into my hand,

31. then whoever comes forth from the doors of my house to meet me, when I return victorious from the Ammonites, shall be the Lord's, and I will offer him up for a burnt offering."

32. So Jephthah crossed over to the Ammonites to fight against them; and the Lord gave them into his hand.

33. And he smote them from Aro'er to the neighborhood of Minnith, twenty cities, and as far as Abel-keramim, with a very great slaughter. So the Ammonites were subdued before the people of Israel.

34. The Jephthah came to his home at Mizpah; and behold, his daughter came out to meet him with timbrels and with dances; she was his only child; beside her he had neither son nor daughter.

35. And when he saw her, he rent his clothes, and said, "Alas, my daughter! you have brought me very low, and you have become the cause of great trouble to me; for I have opened my mouth to the Lord, and I cannot take back my vow."

36. And she said to him, "My father, if you have opened your mouth to the Lord, do to me according to what has gone forth from your mouth, now that the Lord has avenged you on your enemies, on the Ammonites."

37. And she said to her father, "Let this thing be done for me; let me alone two months, that I may go and wander on the mountains, and bewail my virginity, I and my companions."

38. And he said, "Go." And he sent her away for two months: and she departed, she and her companions, and bewailed her virginity upon the mountains.

39. And at the end of two months, she returned to her father, who did with her according to his vow which he had made. She had never known a man. And it became a custom in Israel

40. that the daughters of Israel went year by year to lament the daughter of Jephthah the Gileadite four days in the year. (Judges 12:29–40)

The Jephthah story is essentially a "mirror-image" reversal of the Abraham story, a different arrangement of the same materials.[3] I have diagrammed the two stories in Figure 3.1 in such a way as to bring out their mirror-image qualities. This essentially involves reading the Jephthah story forward and the Abraham story backward (that is, the last

Figure 3.1

Events in the Jephthah Story Placed in One-to-One Correspondence with Events in the Abraham Story

---

JEPHTHAH (read forward)

ABRAHAM (read backward)

1.
Man gives his word to God
[vows]

God gives his word to Man
[promises]

that God will have a dead sacrifice
[sacrifice turns out = his daughter]

that Man will have many live
descendants

if [in future] God gives Man

because [in past] Man gave God

a gift [= God allowed killing of
foreigners]

a gift [= Man is willing to
kill kin/son]

but only daughter replaces animal.

but animal replaces only son.

Thus Man loses only child by
actually killing foreigners.

Thus Man gains many relatives by
potentially killing only child.

2.
Jephthah does slay foreigners.

Abraham starts to slay son.

3.
A child "happens" to come out;
Jephthah's only child replaces
an animal.

A ram "happens" to be there;
the animal replaces Abraham's
only child.

4.
Father tells child that she is
the offering.

Child asks father where the
offering is.

Child tells father to provide
the offering he has promised.

Father assures child that God
will provide the offering He.
wishes

5.
Daughter goes up the mountain
with companions, apart from father.

Father and son go up the
mountain together, leave
companions behind.

6.
Father honors vow [of the past] to
kill only child [daughter].

God commands [future] father
to kill only child [son].

Note: In the Jephthah story read forward from first event to last, and in the
Abraham story read backward from last event to first.

event in the Abraham story corresponds to the first of the Jephthah story, the second-to-last in the Abraham story to the second of the Jephthah story, and so on). The fact that these two stories can be read "back-to-front" against each other is not in itself significant—what it means is that the order of the events in either story is not of paramount importance, rather the symbolic relationship of each event to all the other events in its story is what is of primary importance.

While I cannot give a detailed analysis of these two stories here, it is clear that the same core of "problems" lies behind both of them. One of these problems is surely the nature of one's duties and responsibilities to kin, to fellow humans who are not kin, and to God, as well as how these are to be balanced. Another is the problem of how one adjudicates two moral imperatives when they conflict. The Israelites faced very real conflict between two taboos: on the one hand, they believed that killing people, including "non-kin" (non-Israelites), was wrong; on the other hand, they felt a moral imperative to keep their social identity separate from other groups, through not integrating (for example, not intermarrying) with other groups and through warfare to establish their society within the framework of its historical or mythic narrative (which label—historical or mythic—is appropriate here is a matter of dispute).

In this regard it is interesting that Jephthah, who is only "half" Jewish, kills foreigners, thus valuing kin (his fellow Israelites) above the moral imperative not to kill humans. In this he helps establish Israel but has his own personal line die out (presumably because he killed human beings). Abraham, on the other hand, places God above even kin, and thus not only establishes Israel but has many descendants (in fact, all of Israel).

These two stories clearly manipulate the same elements but arrange them in different configurations. Each story deals with a triangle staked out by God, "man" (father), and sole child (sole legitimate child). In each case, there is a "double vision" in which this triangle can be taken as a set of personal relationships or a set of societal ones in which the child-father-God relationship represents the relationship between Israel, its leaders, and God. Issues of obedience to God, the value one places on kin, the relationship between humans and God, the nature of killing and sacrifice, the relationship between kin and the "whole people," and many others are symbolized and acted out through Jephthah/Abraham; Jephthah's daughter/Isaac; God as silent hearer/God as speaker; Israel as combatant/Israel as God's people. There are, of course, many other arrangements of these elements, other ways to "play with" them in the space of the issues above, other versions of the Abraham/Jephthah–Isaac/Jephthah's daughter story.

And, of course, the New Testament story of Christ is just such a version. In that story, God plays both the role of God and of Abraham/Jephthah; Christ plays the role of Isaac/Jephthah's daughter, the only child of God the father. No animal replaces Christ, and humans (not the father) sacrifice this god/person, and, in that act, humans become spiritual (not material) descendants of God. The Christ story would, of course, make no sense if it were not for the other potential stories in this set, stories like the Abraham–Isaac story and the Jephthah–Jephthah's daughter version of it. By the way, this is why the New Testament can make such plausible claims to having been anticipated by the Old—the New Testament simply tells stories in the same "sets" (within the same "logic") as the Old Testament stories.

There is much more that could be said about these stories. But what is clear is that, while they are narratives, the actual temporal and causal ordering of events is much less important to them than the way in which certain elements (themes), like God, human, kin, non-kin, giving of words, sacrifice, and so forth, are related to each other and fall into a satisfying pattern vis-à-vis each other. We can think of these stories as puzzles in which the same pieces are fit together in different ways but in both cases give a coherent picture (Lévi-Strauss, 1963, 1964–1971, 1966, 1979).

There are other possible arrangements. The meaning of each story resides not just in that story alone, but in the other actual and possible arrangements as well. The problems that these two stories deal with are addressed, not by each story as a single, isolated entity, but rather by combining and juxtaposing the two stories and other variants. Since the set of variants is never closed, the meaning of any story resides in the whole system, which allows many versions to be generated. The system, in turn, resides in the stories themselves as the social group tells them and passes them down through the generations; that is, it resides in the very social practice in which the mythic stories are told and passed down as a mark of the identity of the group. Thus, the meanings of the stories are rooted in history and the social group, not just in the personal mind.

Mythic stories like these don't sit well with our current sense of narrative. They use temporal and causal order to embed themes and events whose juxtaposition and relationships in an imaginary space is much more important than that order itself. They always take on their meaning in relationship to other stories, some of which are in a tradition rooted in the past and some of which are merely potential and arise, if at all, in relation to present exigencies of specific social groups (as did the Christ story). Meaning seeps, so to speak, out of the head and into history and society. And they are "prototypical" in the sense that the society sees them as events and ways of being that can (and ought to be) reenacted in the present.

Where, then, is mythic memory? It resides in a social practice of telling stories of a certain sort (that is, stories that are related to certain stories that have been told in the past) and interpreting them in certain ways (that is, by seeing them as alternative arrangements of similar materials, speaking to the same or similar social, moral, and spiritual problems). Members of the community who play this game must, of course, have something in their heads. They may well have memorized some stories, and they may well have networks of associations (between, for instance, triangles like God-father-heir) that work like generative rules to produce or interpret new versions of old stories.

But this is not the mythic memory, just a set of tools to get in and stay in the game. If someone produces a story or an interpretation of a story that fails to fit the "system"—that is, fails to jell with the social practice as it is carried out and changed through time—then that person's story or interpretation will either change the system/social practice (if it accepted and passed on) or, more likely, will not be accepted, and the person will adapt in the future more fully toward the norms of the social practice. Mythic memory is *in* the social practice that serves as a norm, or a "model," or a "target," that nudges everyone's stories and interpretations toward it, keeping them "in line." The social practice is out in the social interaction, not in people's heads. It can only be studied by studying the world, not the inside of heads.

HISTORY

We can say of history the same thing we have said of myth. Of course, history is a different social practice. And, indeed, history as a social practice is different at different times and in different cultures and in different "scientific" paradigms of historiography. But as in the case of mythic memory, historical memory resides in the social practice. I have argued that myths are interpreted by "stacking" them and seeing a set of stories as alternative arrangements of the same materials speaking to the same problems. They are not unlike the different "weight" configurations across a neural network, each of which we saw is a different "theory" about the relationships the network encodes. Each mythic story in a set is a different "take" on the same set of problems.

Historiography does not "stack" stories but treats any story with different characters and events at different times as *different stories*, necessarily arranged in a sequence and related by complex chains of cause and effect. In historiography, one version of a story is held to be "true" (in historical terms), and the other versions are but versions of what might have happened, how things could have been otherwise. Within this sort of social practice, the Jephthah story cannot be a version of the Abraham-Isaac story; they must be separate realities, connected, if at all, by a chain of cause-effect relations.

However, the basic principle of myth—juxtaposition of alternative versions of the same materials—does operate in historical practices. If we cannot imagine that things could have been otherwise, or if we have no idea what might have happened had a historical actor done things differently, then we are not writing history. The Cuban missile crisis as described (taken as history) only makes sense on the assumption that had the Soviets not withdrawn their missiles, then the United States might very well have gone to war. Without this assumption, it wasn't a "crisis." But this story, the one that didn't happen, is just another rearrangement of the Cuban missile materials, a reworking that gives the original ("real") version a large part of its meaning. In fact, historians very often carry out debate about which versions of a historical episode are "correct," by debating which "what if" alternate stories are "correct," and this is obviously nothing about which we can have "actual evidence" in terms of "real-world" happenings.

Of course, people argue over what is history and what is myth; these are just arguments over which social practice a story more properly belongs in. For example, some people argue that the Abraham and Isaac story is history, which is just to say that it is then thought to have taken place in historical time, and the reporter (or repeater) of the story contracts a different set of responsibilities because he or she has entered a different social practice. For instance, the reporter (or repeater) takes on the responsibility to "empirically" relate the story to other historical narratives, not just other mythic ones (where the meaning of "empirical" is determined by the sort of historiography one has allegiance to as a social practice). The story will stay pretty much the same, though not necessarily exactly so. For instance, in some forms of historiography, the name "God" in the story will have to be replaced by something like "what Abraham believed to be the voice of God," because God cannot be an historical actor in some theories of history. And of course, one can attempt to argue that the Abraham and Isaac story is properly part of both social practices, myth and history (as is, for instance, much of the Abraham Lincoln story in the United States—see Schwartz, 1990).

Historical memory, like myth, resides *not* in stories in the head, nor in books or documents, nor in "real happenings" in the world. History is, as much as myth, an open and generative system, though people don't often think of history in this way. New versions of historical episodes arise, versions which reflect later happenings, and not just the historical events themselves. The historiographical practices of a group determine whether these new versions "fit" within the practice (or whether the practice will be changed to accommodate them). If they don't fit, and the practice doesn't change to accommodate them, then they aren't history, aren't part of historical memory. Once again, then, historical memory is *in* the social practice (and, of course, some historiographies believe that the practice of historical accounts over time gives rise to closer and closer approximations to what "actually" happened).

To see how history operates as an open and generative system, consider, for instance, the Muslim view of the 'Crusades,' a set of events that "happened" between the end of the eleventh and the end of the thirteenth centuries. My discussion here is based on the work of Paul Connerton (1989, 15–16). Connerton argues that medieval Muslim historians did not share with medieval European Christians the sense of witnessing a great struggle between Islam and Christendom for the control of the Holy Land. In the extensive Muslim historiography of that time, he points out, the words "Crusade" and "Crusader" do not occur. Medieval Muslim historians spoke of the Crusaders either as the "Infidels" or as the "Franks," and they viewed the attacks launched by them in Syria, Egypt, and Mesopotamia, between the end of the eleventh and the end of the thirteenth centuries, as being in no way fundamentally different from the former wars waged between Islam and the Infidels: in Syria itself in the course of the tenth century and before, in Andalus throughout the Spanish Reconquista, and in Sicily against the Normans.

But in the period since 1945 an expanding body of Arabic historical writing has taken the Crusades as its theme. The "Crusades" have now become a code word for the malign intentions of the Western powers. Muslim historians have come to see a certain parallelism between the period of the twelfth and thirteenth centuries and the last hundred years. In both cases the Islamic Middle East was assailed by European forces which succeeded in imposing their control upon a large part of the region. From a Muslim viewpoint, the Crusades have come to be seen as the primary phase of European colonization, the prefiguration of a long-term movement that includes the Bonaparte expedition, the British conquest of Egypt, and the Mandate system in the Levant. That movement is seen as culminating in the foundation of the state of Israel; and with each ensuing struggle—the Arab-Israel War of 1948, the Suez War, the Six Day War—the Muslim study of the Crusades gained momentum. Muslim historians now see in the rise and fall of the Crusader principalities parallels to contemporary events. The Crusaders, who crossed the sea and established an independent state in Palestine, have become proto-Zionists. One story has replaced the other as what "really" happened, and it is the fact that both stories are tellable, and even viewable as alternative arrangements of the same sorts of materials, that allows either one to make any sense.

Exactly the same sort of thing can be seen if we consider Western histories of the Crusades. Here my discussion is based on the work of Paul Johnson (1976, 241–45): we get several alternate stories across time, reflecting things that have happened since the Crusades. According to Johnson, Western historians have argued that three factors combined to produce the Crusades. These factors are really three different stories out of which different "master narratives" can be made up, depending upon how you integrate the three stories.

The first factor was the development of small-scale "holy wars" against the Muslims in the Spanish theater. In 1063, Ramiro I, King of Aragon, was murdered by a Muslim, and Pope Alexander II promised an indulgence for all who fought for the cross to revenge the atrocity.

There was, second, a Frankish tradition, dating from around 800, that the Carolingian monarch had a right and a duty to protect the Holy Places in Jerusalem and the Western pilgrims who went there. This was acknowledged by the Muslim caliphs, who until the late eleventh century preferred Frankish interference to what they regarded as the far more dangerous penetration by Byzantium. From the tenth century, armed Western pilgrimages grew in frequency and size—in 1064–66, for instance, 7,000 Germans, many armed, traveled together to Jerusalem.

A third factor, however, was the vast increase in Western population in the eleventh and twelfth centuries, and the consequent land hunger. Pioneer farming at the frontiers was one solution. Another was the almost unconscious decision, at the end of the eleventh century, to marry the Spanish idea of conquering land from the infidel with the practice of the mass, armed pilgrimage to the Holy Land. Peter the Hermit led a mob of 20,000 men, women, and children, including, in all likelihood, many families carrying all their worldly goods with them. Most of these people were very poor; they had been unable to obtain land or agricultural work during a prolonged labor surplus. They intended to settle in the Holy

Land, as did, in fact, many of the knights, most of whom had no money or lands.

So now what do we say of medieval Western people trekking to the Holy Land? Were they immigrants, armed pilgrims, holy warriors fighting for a seat in heaven, all three, different things at different times? Was the answer different for different people, perhaps for different people in the same horde moving to the Holy Land? All we can do is structure a story combining these elements in certain ways, assemble our documents to support it (if that is part of our historiographical practice), relate it other "historical events" in sequence, and hope that our story is at least accepted as a "historical" one, if not as the "right" one.

If it is not accepted as a historical narrative, then we will have to change our way of telling such stories. Our stories and what's in our head don't take precedence, the social practice does (which is not to say we can't change the social practice). Apart from such stories, the "Crusader" standing on the sands of the "Holy Land" is nothing and nowhere—a meaningless "datum" related to billions of other such data. Historical memory is in the social historiographical practice that nudges our "play" in the history game toward the "norms" of the social practice; it is not in our heads or in the world of real events outside social practices of human groups. And, as with myth, one can't do history—have a historical memory—alone.

PERSONAL MEMORY

Personal memory, though, once again a different social practice than either myth or history (and one that is itself different in different cultures and at different times in a single culture), is, like history and myth, *in* the social practice, not in the head or the world outside the social practices of human groups. As in history, accounts of personal memories are sequenced and not stacked; as in history any account makes sense only against alternative versions of the account that serve as "what would have happened if" versions. Personal memories differ from history in that they must be sequenced with other stories that we take to be about the self and to constitute its biography or "career" (Goldschmidt, 1990).

Any social group has ways of emplotting episodes of experience that count as memories and ways of relating these episodes to life biographies or "career trajectories" (Belenky, Clinchy, Goldberger, & Tarule, 1986; Gilligan, 1986). If your account diverges too far from this practice, the practice will nudge you back toward its norm, or change to accommodate you. In either case, the norms within the social practice—what count as proper plots—constitute memory, not what is "stored" in your head.

Like history and myth, personal memory is an open and generative system that comes to reflect ever-changing circumstances and not just the past. Indeed, one of the purposes of psychotherapy is to get the patient to see that his or her memories can be given new episodic structures and a new set of plots. The patient changes, in some regard, his or allegiance to social practices, accepting the psychologist's social practice to an extent. This changes the patient's memories.

In the following chapters much discussion will exemplify the point that accounts of personal experience are embedded in allegiances to different social practices and change as these social practices change. Thus, I will not elaborate this point further here. The point I want to end on here is, rather, that mythic memory, historical memory, and personal memory name things that exist in social practices, not in heads, books, or the world apart from what human groups say and do. What is in books, the world, and heads are merely tools. One can, indeed, pump a small piece of metal into someone else's body with a gun, causing them to die, but one can only murder, assassinate, kill in a gang "drive-by" shooting, or capitally punish someone by being part of a social practice. Apart from the social practice one can do none of these things. Therefore, the murder, assassination, "gang drive-by shooting," or capital punishment is in the practice, not in the gun, the persons alone, or the world apart from the social practice. So too our memories.

NOTES

1. Any verb in a sentence, together with its associated nominals and modifiers, constitutes a clause. Thus, a sentence like "While John was *drinking*, Mary *whispered* to Sue that he *was* a fool" (where the "main verb" is italicized in each clause) contains three clauses: (1) John was drinking; (2) Mary whispered to Sue that . . . ; (3) he was a fool. Clause 1 is subordinated to what follows it ("Mary whispered to Sue that he was a fool"); clause 3 ("he was a fool") is embedded inside clause 2 ("Mary whispered to Sue that . . . "). Clause 2 ("Mary whispered to Sue that . . . ") is the "main clause" in the sentence as a whole (it is unsubordinated to and unembedded in any other clause). A sentence with only one main verb (such as "Mary whispered something to Sue") is both a clause and a (simple) sentence.

2. Thus, in the example sentence in note 1, "While John was *drinking*, Mary *whispered* to Sue that he *was* a fool," with its three clauses, the clause "Mary whispered to Sue that . . . " could be a foregrounded clause in a narrative. It is the main clause of its sentence, contains a "real verb" that

names an action, and states this verb in the simple past tense (*whispered*). The other two clauses in this sentence do not have all these properties. The first ("John was drinking") is not the main clause in the sentence (since it is subordinated to "Mary whispered to Sue that . . . "), and it is not in the simple past tense. The third ("he was a fool") is also not the main clause in the sentence, since it is subordinated to the preceding clause ("Mary whispered to Sue that . . . "), and its verb ("was") does not name an action. If this sentence was in a narrative, it would foreground the fact that Mary whispered something to Sue. If we wanted to foreground John's being foolish, we could rewrite the sentence in a variety of ways, including: "While drinking, John behaved so foolishly that Mary whispered to Sue that he was a fool" (now "John behaved so foolishly that . . . " is the main clause, and "Mary whispered to Sue that . . . " is embedded inside it).

3. The approach I take to biblical texts is best exemplified in the work of Edmund Leach; see Leach (1967, 1976) and Leach and Aycock (1983). I believe it was a paper by Leach that first, years ago, called my attention to these texts, but I can no longer recover the source. Wanda Giles has brought to my attention the important point that the son/daughter difference in the two stories is not innocent. Girls and women do not, by and large, fare well in the Bible. The modern reader (and probably also the original audience), within the logic of biblical stories, is certainly not surprised to find that the daughter dies, while the son lives. This is also a good example of how the elements that are inserted into the inversions and transformations of the mythic stories are themselves value-ladened and thematically meaningful.

4

SOUL

Psychology is the discipline that studies the workings of the human mind. In the last chapter, I argued that there can be no viable study of the mind that does not focus on *social practices*, rather than on what is inside people's heads. This is a striking claim only because American psychology has so long focused on "computerlike" computations carried out inside the head, rather than on what people say and do in the world of physical action and social interaction.

I have argued thus far that so-called "mental activities," like memory or reading a text, are, in reality, not in the head, but in the social practices of socioculturally defined groups of people. What is in people's heads are *tools* they put to use in engaging in these social practices, much as the body is used as a tool to play baseball, along with bats and balls. But bodies, bats and balls are not the game of baseball. To restrict the study of baseball to a study of bodies, bats, and balls, would surely miss most of the interesting things there are to say about baseball (though, of course, not all of them). Similarly, to study the insides of heads misses most (though not all) of the interesting things there are to be said about "mental activities."

The chapter will state a view about how what is inside the head relates to what is outside it (the physical world and social practices). I will argue that there are four things at stake in the study of any mental phenomenon, two of these (a and b below) are, indeed, inside the head, and two are not (c and d below): (a) networks of associations of the sort we looked at in Chapter 2 above; (b) "folk theories" about the domain these associations cover (for example, memory, reading, judging, classifying, speaking, and so on); (c) scientific principles about the domain these associations cover; and, finally, (d) social practices in the service of which people put to use their networks of associations and their folk theories. Psychology ought to be the study of these four things and their interrelationships. As such, it is only in part the study of what is in the head.

In this chapter I will argue that it is one of the consequences of the view of mind and society developed in this book that it is strikingly unlikely that what we believe about ourselves in our everyday lives is, in any helpful sense, "true." In fact, I will argue that "self-deception" (though this is not to be taken, in every case, as negative) is the basis of human intelligence.

FIRST, A NOTE ON FREUD

A part of the worldview of the discipline of psychology, at least as practiced in the United States, can be seen clearly if we consider standard English translations of Freud (Bettelheim, 1982; see also Goldschmidt, 1990, 65–67). Where Freud used everyday German terms, English translations use Latin names. For instance, "womb" (*Mutterleib*) becomes *uterus* and "lustful watching" (*Schaulust*) becomes *scopophilia*. More significantly, Freud did not write his three most familiar words— "id," "ego," and "superego"—in Latin. Rather, he wrote: *das Ich* (the I), *das Es* (the it), and *das Uber-Ich* (the over-I). Finally, and yet more importantly, where Freud used the word "soul" (*Seele*), the translators regularly substituted *mind*.

These translations constitute a rewriting of Freud. Freud viewed "the I," "the it," and "the over-I" in terms of a conflict internal to the human soul. On the other hand, American Freudians view the ego, id, and superego as the topography/geography of the mind, much as the founders of the American study of "intelligence" (for example, Charles Spearman, Edward Thorndike, and L. L. Thurstone) treated intelligence as a geography of the mind in which various "mental abilities" constituted the landscape of the mind (Sternberg, 1990). The move from Freud's words to the translators' words constitutes a shift from an exploration of emotional turmoil to an exploration of "mental problems"—a transition from healing spiritual malaise to treating mental disorder.

The move from Freud's words to the translators' also represents the transformation of psychoanalysis into a branch of medicine. According to Bruno Bettelheim, Freud did not desire this transformation. Bettelheim quotes Freud as saying that he wanted to "protect" analysis from physicians as well as from priests: "I want to entrust it to a profession that doesn't yet exist, a profession of secular ministers of souls, who don't have to be physicians and must not be priests" (1982, 62). What Freud wanted for psychoanalysis was, in fact, a *secular ministry*.

In the early part of this century, American psychoanalysts argued that the practice of psychoanalysis ought to be limited to physicians. The issue nearly split the International Psycho-Analytical Association until a compromise was worked out in 1932. The compromise allowed each national society to determine its own qualifications for membership, and American analysts proceeded to determine, against Freud's convictions, that only physicians could become analysts. American psychoanalysts wanted no part of a "secular soul." Rather, they wanted to borrow the high prestige of both medicine and science by "treating" the mind, in the way in which a physician treats the body. And just as the body has organs that can get "sick" and become poorly adjusted to other organs, so too the mind has parts that can be sick and maladjusted.

But what might the *soul* be? Many religious people believe that each human individual is *ensouled* by a divine force. Freud believed human beings were ensouled thanks to their *socialization* early in life. The emotional turmoil of the I, the it, and the over-I is an embodiment of the social turmoil of the child and her early social environment. We need not accept Freud's views of early socialization to appreciate the relevance of social practices to individual identity.

I will define the soul—much as Bourdieu (1984, 1990) defines *habitus*—as the mental structures through which an individual perceives and appreciates the physical and social world. A soul is achieved through the experience each uniquely endowed individual has of holding various "positions" in social space, the space of families, ethnic and other socioculturally defined groups, and various social institutions like schools, jobs, and governments (Bourdieu, 1990, 130–31). It is an internalization of the structures of the social world, and it can be built upon contradiction, tension, and instability, whence the need for the secular ministry of psychotherapists.

NOW, ON TO BIRDS

Bird watching, it turns out, can throw light on the matter of the soul. Every good bird-watcher acquires a "sixth sense" about what kinds of birds and how many different kinds will be found in a given piece of habitat. Bird-watchers cannot, however, explain how they know this. This is not to say that they won't try: but what they will offer as an explanation is their "folk theory" (Holland & Quinn, 1987) about what determines the diversity of bird species in a given area.[1]

The folk theory need not be correct for the bird-watchers' practices to work successfully, since the practices do not in actuality (completely) follow the folk theory. The folk theory is simply a rationalization of the practice. It turns out, as we will see below, that the part of the mind that constructs such folk theories does not have access to the part of the mind that directs the practice of which the folk theory is a theory (P. S. Churchland, 1986; Gazzaniga, 1985). This is certainly *not* to say that the bird-watcher's folk theory isn't important. It may be very important, indeed. Bird-watchers may very well judge other bird-watchers on whether they have allegiance to the folk theory, and bird-watchers organize large parts of their social practice (clubs, newsletters, trips, and so forth) around it.

The great ecologist of animal communities, Robert MacArthur, developed a measure that in a limited way duplicates what most bird-watchers can do without thinking: predict the number of bird species living in a given habitat (MacArthur, 1972; see Erlich, 1986, 211–12). Like most scientists, MacArthur used an intuition from the bird-watcher's folk theory to get his scientific theory started (an example of what Peirce, 1940—see also Hanson, 1958—called "abduction"). He made an initial guess that the vertical pattern of the vegetation in an area was important. After all, birds are often thought of as typically occurring either in open fields or in woodland, and the most obvious difference between these two environments is that the vegetation is taller in one than the other.

MacArthur developed a quantitative index of the vertical structure of vegetation in various habitats, which he called "the index of foliage height diversity." This index is a simple measure of the variation in the proportion of foliage occurring at different heights above the ground. The details of the index are not important here, but it yields a single number that is low if all of the foliage is found at a single level regardless of height (as in a treeless field of grass or a woodland with no undergrowth) and high if about the same amount of vegetation is found at several different heights above the ground (herbs, bushes, and trees growing intermixed).

MacArthur then used his index to discover a simple principle for accurately predicting bird species diversity from a knowledge of foliage height diversity: the greater the foliage height diversity, the greater the number of bird species. Oddly enough, the diversity of plant species does not itself influence how many bird species are present, except to the extent that it influences foliage height diversity. It does not matter, for example, whether a dense forest canopy is formed by one or five species of trees. What does matter is whether these trees so block out the light that no bushes can grow beneath them.

Now, we can note some salient differences between a careful, scientific, MacArthurian measurer out in the forest and a first-rate birdwatcher. The scientist can do only laboriously what a first-rate birder can do at a glance: predict how many bird species will be found in a given habitat. But the scientist can state the general principle involved; the birder cannot. The scientist can tell an inexperienced person how to predict how many species of birds there will be in a given area; the birder cannot. On the other hand, the birder will find lots of birds; the scientist may very well actually find none.

There is a mistake regularly committed by psychologists that we might be tempted to make about bird watching. We might be tempted to say that the principle ("rule") MacArthur discovered is *in* the birder's head, and that it is *in virtue of* this principle (a part of the birder's "competence," we might be tempted to say) that the birder ("unconsciously") knows how many species of birds will be found in a given area. This is a paradigmatic instance of what Pierre Bourdieu calls the *scholastic fallacy*: "this fallacy, encouraged by the situation of *schole*, leisure and school, induces [people] to think that agents involved in action, in practice, in life, think, know and see as someone who has the leisure to think thinks, knows and sees, as the scientist whose mode of thought presupposes leisure both in its genesis and its functioning . . . " (1990, 112; see also Bourdieu, 1984).

MacArthur's principle need not be in—and almost certainly isn't in—the heads of bird-watchers, consciously or unconsciously. So what is in their heads? According to the view of the mind developed in Chapters 2 and 3 above (a so-called connectionist view; see Allman, 1989; P. M. Churchland, 1989; P. S. Churchland, 1986; Clark, 1989; Johnson, 1991; Johnson & Brown, 1988; McClelland, Rumelhart, & the PDP Research Group, 1986; Rumelhart, McClelland, & the PDP Research Group, 1986), all that is in our bird-watchers' heads are *associations* among various features of objects and events that our bird-watchers have experienced.

Thus, we all recognize birds because a great many features—feathers, flying, beaks, certain ways of perching and walking, and so on—are variously associated with each other to various degrees of strength. They are associated in such a way that seeing or thinking about one or more such features brings to mind—more or less strongly—all the others. Of course, the networks of associations in birders' heads are much richer, more detailed, and more complex (for example, a white rump is associated with birds of types X, Y, and Z, and no others).

Good birders form expectations about the diversity of bird species they will see in a given environment, in part through the complex array of associations among types of habitats and species of birds that exists in their heads thanks to their past experiences. These associations are by no means simple. A given birder may expect to see birds of type X in a given habitat because she has frequently seen them when those sorts of bushes over there have been present, but then, there was that very salient experience when that sort of configuration of trees and water over there contained birds of type Y, and the birder has never seen birds of type Y and type X in the same place. Frequency, salience, and the absence of certain experiences all play a role.

The birder need have no grand generalizations, like MacArthur's principle, in her head in order to successfully find a great many birds. An environment with lots of variably heighted perches (which, thus, happens to have a high MacArthurian foliage height diversity index) will set off many associations for the birder—will relate to many past experiences and their network of associations with the features of other experiences—and lead the birder to expect a good number of different types of birds. The birder may believe that it is the diversity of species of plants that leads to the bird diversity, but this mistaken belief will not necessarily affect the success of her bird-watching practice, especially as there is some (though not a perfect) correlation between plant species diversity and foliage height diversity.

There is no reason to believe (and good reason not to believe) that birders have conscious access to the network of associations that are in their minds (P. S. Churchland, 1986; Gazzaniga, 1985). But birders do have something else in their heads beyond these associations. They have various versions of a folk theory of birds, bird watching, and bird species diversity within habitats. This is something they can use in their talk about birds and to answer questions about their practice.

How do birders get this theory? Since they have no conscious access to their networks of associations, which partially guide their bird-watching practice in the field, they did not get their versions of the folk theory by inspecting their mental networks. They got it, rather, both by inspecting their actual practice (their overt behaviors) and through association with other birders in the social practice of bird watching.

The folk theory need not be wrong—the group could have read MacArthur's work—but it need not be right either. The folk theory *also* contributes to the birder's expectations about which birds will be seen where. Thus, the actual practice of bird-watchers is a construct of their network of associations and their folk theories (which, thus, sometimes get circularly confirmed). Folk theories can also affect practice by telling new birders where and how to *focus* their observations. This, in turn, helps determine which aspects of new birders' experiences will get into their networks of associations, and thus helps determine (though by no means fully so) the nature of their mental networks.

We might say that the birder's mental network is the *id* of her bird-watching self, her folk theory is the *ego* of her bird-watching self, and principles like MacArthur's are the *superego* of her bird-watching self to the extent that she is aware of them. Folk theories do not immediately collapse in front of scientific theories; they engage in various sorts of collusion and resistance, not unlike struggles between the ego and the superego (Atran, 1990; Desmond, 1989; Douglas, 1986). And, furthermore, sometimes scientific theories—and much of psychology is a sad case in point—are in large part just folk theories dressed up in formal garb (P. S. Churchland, 1986; P. M. Churchland, 1989).

So we have mental networks of associations, folk theories, and scientific theories. However, there is something over, above, and beyond these three. There is also *the social practice* of bird watching. To confuse this with the other three things is a large mistake, though, once again, the sort of mistake regularly made by psychologists. Bird watching (in the sense of "birding") is certainly not in people's heads, nor is it in their acts of looking at birds in fields and woods. It is a set of ongoing activities and interactions among birders—ways of talking, acting, watching, interacting, reading, and writing, with associated meetings, written materials, bird reserves, associations, and physical settings for meetings and materials.

Such a social practice with its associated people and things I refer to as a "Discourse," with a capital D (Gee, 1989a, 1990c). I use the term "Discourse" (with a capital D) to make clear that I am talking about something that *means* (*discourses*) though it is not in any one person's head, but rather an amalgam of language, bodies, heads, and various props in the world (like birds and books). My use of the term is obviously related in various ways to Foucault's work (for example, Foucault, 1980—see also Macdonell, 1986; and Gee, 1990c).

The Discourse of bird watching has several functions, among which are the following: (1) it serves to *apprentice* new birders, (2) it helps *form folk theories* about birds, habitats, and bird watching, and (3) it *keeps everyone's mental networks of associations* in regard to birds, habitats, and bird watching *"pretty much" alike* by ensuring that they hold relatively similar folk theories, have many experiences of relevantly similar sorts, and focus on the "right" parts of that experience. If your mental network (which is never identical to anyone else's) gets too much "out of line," or your folk theory deviates too far from that of others, your practice will begin to render you marginal to the Discourse, and the Discourse will "discipline" you and put you back in line, or you will cease to be a birder.

This discipline can, of course, take a great many forms, including diverse interactions with other birders, references in conversations and publications, and the workings of the physical world, which is, of course, part of the Discourse. In fact, aspects of the social practice and the physical world often play a more important role in birders' sightings than anything going on in their brains or eyes. If a birder has not followed the "rules" for ethical claims in having sighted a rare bird, it hasn't ("officially") been "seen," and it cannot go on the birder's list. And the presence or absence (through extinction, for example) of rare birds in the world has a great deal to do with what birders can claim to have sighted or not, certainly more (or, at least, not less) than any chemical reaction going on in their brains (claims to have sighted extinct birds are disciplined severely by the Discourse). The social practice and the physical world structure the activity of bird watching as much as or more than the nature of the human brain. To study only the latter and ignore the former would leave one with a quite silly view of the nature of bird watching.

If one were interested in constructing a theory of bird watching, then it would be imperative to be clear about what we were studying: mental networks, folk theories, scientific principles, or the Discourse. And we would have to primarily focus our attention on the Discourse as the device in and through which mental networks and folk theories are formed, adjusted, and regulated, and which serves as the mediator for any scientific principles that will eventually affect members of the Discourse. When psychology studies a phenomenon like memory, for example, it typically confuses these elements, ignores Discourses as not "mental," and attributes principles, rules, or computations it discovers about phenomena relevant to a Discourse to the minds of its members, thereby committing the "scholastic fallacy."

MIND AND SOCIETY

Now, I have discussed bird watching at such length because we theorists of the mind are much less emotionally caught up in this activity than we are with things like meaning, literacy, language learning, reading, and memory. However, I want to claim that what I have said about the study of birding applies also to the study of these activities.

Take memory, which we discussed in length in the last chapter—say, my memories of a loved one's death. What is in my head in regard to this experience is not some neatly "stored" little mental movie or mental short story with a discrete beginning, ending, and plot, though much psychological work on memory would make us believe this. What is in my head is a complex set of associations among features and properties of the people, events, and objects involved in this experience and in other experiences, events, people, and so on related to it. These complex associations do not come cut up as "episodes" with neat beginnings and ends and plots. Rather, in the *reporting* of this memory, or some aspect of it, I *impose* with due regard for the context of the reporting and my current purposes an *episodic structure* on pieces of my mental network of associations, with a beginning, an end, and various foregroundings and backgroundings. I *emplot* my experience, differently on different occasions.

There are folk theories about memory and the mind (D'Andrade, 1987). For example, the view that memory is like a picture or movie in the mind, that memories fade like old photographs, and so forth, are pieces of common folk theories of memory in our culture. Unfortunately, the discipline of psychology has too often traded on these folk theories in its construction of a "scientific" theory of the mind. Much psychological theorizing is just a fancy formalization of folk theories of the mind. The connectionist view of the mind assumes these folk theories are not accurate and, thus too, assumes that large parts of current psychological theories are wrong.

Finally, just as in the case of birding, there are social practices in regard to reporting and evaluating memories, social practices which, in fact, vary across cultures (Connerton, 1989; Middleton & Edwards, 1990). These practices constitute Discourses or play a role in a number of them. They are constituted by the characteristic ways in which culturally, socially, and historically defined groups of people talk about, interact over, appreciate, and evaluate memories, which include, of course, characteristic ways of episodically emplotting reports of experience. Like bird watching, these group-oriented ways of "doing memory" apprentice newcomers (usually children), helping them to establish their mental networks of associations. They also help everyone in the group to keep their networks in line with other people in the group, and they establish, regulate, and maintain folk theories about memory and the mind. And, once again, these practices are not in the mind.

This means, of course, that in studying memory, we are focusing our study on something *out in the social world of interaction and physical settings*, not something primarily in anyone's head. Our networks, and whatever else is in our heads, are *tools* with which we can get in and play "memory games"; they are tools with which to play the Discourse. Psychology regularly mistakes the tools that build buildings with the buildings they build. Memories are, in reality, what Discourses license as types of reports of past experience, not anything in the head.

The same can be said of reading or any type of literacy (school science, literature, law, mathematics, and so forth through many more; see Gee 1989a, 1990c). We read by having certain things in our heads (tools) that allow us to participate in diverse sorts of social activities—that is, in Discourses (different types of literacy—Cook-Gumperz, 1986; Gee, 1987). These social activities help establish what is in our heads, form our folk theories about reading and meaning, and keep us in line with the practice. Scientists can discover principles about reading (for example, nice generalizations about the relationship between the written and spoken codes encapsulated in principles of phonics). But these principles need not be in people's heads as they read. Neither need they be the basic guide to informing educational practice in producing readers.

If we want to study reading, we must focus on one of the many literacy Discourses. And this is to focus on the world of social practices, that is, people and things in relationships, not on heads. Since things like meaning, reading, and memory are what psychology studies, then psychology is not, I argue, primarily the study of heads, but of the social world. If psychotherapists minister to the soul, then cognitive psychologists should study—and help to change—the social world that either helps or harms the souls of, for example, children in schools.

FOLK THEORIES

So far I have argued that in the study of any "mental phenomenon"— we can take *memory* or *reading* as an example—we must distinguish among: (1) networks of associations in the head, as well as other information-processing tools that help people engage in social practices; (2) folk theories that people pick up as part of apprenticeships in particular social practices and continue to develop as part of their ongoing engagement in those practices; (3) scientific theories relevant to the same or a similar domain as particular folk theories—the principles of such scientific theories need not be in the heads of people engaged in the social practices, but they can affect those practices and their associated folk theories because people in the practices can read (or hear about) the scientific theories and understand them to various degrees (just as scientists can "steal from" and variously "clean up" various folk theories); and (4) the social practices themselves each seen as a particular *Discourse*, that is, as an amalgam of ways of acting, interacting, talking, valuing, and thinking, with associated objects, settings, and events, which are characteristic of people whose social practice it is.

Above I argued that the part of the mind that constructs folk theories does not have access to the part of the mind that contains the network of associations which, in part, direct the practice of which the folk theory is a theory. Thus, our bird-watcher has stored up an immense quantity of associations among features of birds, habitats, and times of day (among other things), and these determine in part what the bird-watcher will expect and where she will look for birds. Her folk theory about birds and bird watching is not, however, formed by directly inspecting her mental networks—the mind is built in such a way that she cannot inspect these networks. The networks are *encapsulated* from other, more "conscious," parts of the mind (I will argue this case further below).

The networks of the mind fall into various modules (subsystems), each of which carries out specific tasks. These modules carry out their work, and the more conscious part of the mind is aware of the "results" of this work, at least in the sense that the person can and does carry out actions on the basis of such results (looks for birds in a certain type of habitat). But the "computations" the modules carry out (the sorts of activation that occur across their many systems of neurons) are not open to conscious awareness. In that sense, we don't know *why* our minds have chosen to "recommend" a certain expectation or course of action. All we can do, it turns out, is "speculate" on the matter—in much the same way any one else would speculate about why we had expected or done something—by considering what we actually expect and do (Cialdini, 1984; Langer, 1989). We are not really in a privileged position vis-à-vis our own expectations and actions, except that we have usually had more experience observing our own expectations and actions than others have. This sort of speculation about the expectations and actions of others and ourselves (which, of course, always seems to us in regard to our own case much more "certain" and "obvious" than it deserves to be) is the process by which we formulate our folk theories.

This speculation is inherently *social* in that different social and cultural groups build folk theories in quite different ways. You are not going to

consider—even as an explication of your own behavior—any "explana-
tory hypothesis" that none of the sociocultural groups to which you
belong considers "possible" (or, rather, you may, but you won't remain
long a valued member of the sociocultural group whose norms you have
broken, and you will feel pressure either to give up your view or work
to change the viewpoint of the other members of the group).

The claim that we "make up" theories about what we do without access
to the actual "computations" our minds have carried out, leaving us only
to speculate on our actions, emotions, and behaviors, has crucial
implications for the nature of human sense making and for the nature of
human cultures and social groups. Thus, I now turn to a more detailed
consideration of the nature of the mind/brain that underlies this claim. I
will draw my evidence first from neurobiology and then from the recent
work on the evolutionary development of human intelligence.

SPLIT-BRAIN PATIENTS AND THE INTERPRETER
IN THE BRAIN

The human brain—as everyone now knows from wildly overstated
popular claims about "right-brain" and "left-brain" styles and differences—possesses two cerebral cortexes, hemispheres, or half-brains. The
left cortex, or hemisphere, or half-brain, controls the right half of the
body and is the part of the brain that usually controls language and general
cognitive functions. The right cortex, or hemisphere, or half-brain, does
not normally contribute to language processing in any major way. The
right hemisphere controls the left half of the body, and it usually manages
nonverbal processes, such as attention and subtle pattern discrimination
like facial recognition and line orientation, and in the auditory domain
it controls such things as detecting the difference between complex tones.
Normally these two parts of the brain are interconnected through the
corpus collosum. This single nerve fiber system constitutes the largest
neural pathway in the animal world. It keeps each hemisphere aware of
the activities of the other. As far as we can tell, it is a totally efficient
reporting system. Thus, to discuss any normal person as "left-brained"
or "right-brained" is meaningless.

Research on what the two hemispheres of the brain do or do best has
been greatly aided by work on so-called split-brain patients (much of my
account in the early parts of this section is indebted to P. S. Churchland's
excellent overview of the issues in *Neurophilosophy: Toward a Unified
Science of the Mind/Brain*). These are patients who have had the nerve
fibers connecting their two hemispheres surgically sectioned, usually

because they have been victims of severe epilepsy. For reasons not completely understood, disconnecting the two hemispheres can serve as a treatment for this disease. Once the two halves of the brain are disconnected, researchers can detect a subtle disunity in the cognitive lives of split-brain patients, a disunity that raises deep philosophical questions about the nature and unity of the self and throws important light on the sorts of "stories" we "normals" tell ourselves (P. S. Churchland, 1986; Dennett, 1984).

In one typical experiment with split-brain patients (Gazzaniga and LeDoux, 1978), visual information is sent exclusively to the right hemisphere (by controlling where and how the visual information hits the eyes) and then a question is posed to see whether this information is available to the left hemisphere. For example, the subject fixates on the midpoint of a visual display, and a tachistoscope is used to flash a signal to the left visual hemifield of each eye for a designated period, roughly 200 milliseconds. Thanks to the way the eyes and brain are hooked up, this has the effect of sending the visual information only to the right hemisphere (in a normal *or* split-brain patient—remember that the right hemisphere controls the left side of the body and, thus, the left "side" of each eye).

In this type of setup, if the word "spoon" is flashed to the right hemisphere and the subject is asked to report what he saw, he answers "nothing." The patient answers "nothing" because, in the usual case, speaking is a left-hemisphere function, and the left hemisphere has, indeed, seen nothing (the information was sent to the right hemisphere). Thanks to the fact that the connection between the patient's right and left hemispheres has been severed, the right hemisphere cannot pass over the information as to what it saw to the left hemisphere.

However, if the patient is asked to use his left hand (which, again thanks to how the brain is hooked to the body, is controlled by the right hemisphere) to feel under a cloth for the object seen, the left hand picks out a spoon. The right hemisphere, capable of controlling motor acts and in control of the left hand, can act on the information it has seen (though it cannot talk about it through the use of speech). Hence, the right hemisphere "knows" what it has seen, and the left hand acts on the information. On the other hand, the left hemisphere knows nothing and hence, being the linguistically fluent hemisphere, says it knows nothing. Such cases give rise to interesting and important philosophical questions. For example, does this patient *know* or *not know* that he has seen a fork? Does he have "two minds," one of which knows and the other of which doesn't? Does he have two "selves"?

There is, in fact, substantial individual variation in capacities of split-brain patients (Gazzaniga, 1983)—most split-brain patients give virtually no responses at all to stimuli presented to the right hemisphere, not even to simple perceptual matching tests like that above (where the patient saw a picture of a spoon and then picked up a spoon with his hand). And, in uncommon cases, certain patients have right hemispheres that can, to a certain degree, comprehend language. Two patients studied by Michael Gazzaniga and his colleagues had striking right-hemisphere capacities, not only for linguistic comprehension but also for some linguistic expression (Gazzaniga and LeDoux 1978, Gazzaniga 1983). Since the right hemisphere of these patients can comprehend language, researchers can carry out a wider array of tasks with them. Such patients allow researchers to investigate how the left hemisphere of a split-brain patient thinks about the behavior intended not by it, but by right hemisphere (intentions to which the left hemisphere has no access in spit-brain patients).

The answer is fascinating and disquieting at the same time: it turns out that the left hemisphere does *not* go through a conscious process of seeing behavior intended by the right hemisphere as uncaused by it, wondering how it happened, and then deliberately fabricating an explanation. Nor does it claim to be unable to explain it. Rather, it smoothly and effortlessly incorporates the behavior into its own scheme of things, providing a coherent and plausible explanation, without puzzlement or any apparent attempt to lie. Consider the following well-known example (much of the following discussion is based on Michael Gazzaniga's book *The Social Brain: Discovering the Networks of the Mind*).

A different picture is flashed to each hemisphere. For example, a picture of a snowy scene is flashed to the right hemisphere, and a picture of a chicken's claw is flashed to the left one. Then, a separate array of pictures is placed before the subject—say, pictures of a lawn mower, a rake, a shovel, an ax, an apple, a toaster, a hammer, and a chicken's head. The patient is asked to select with each hand a picture that best matches the flashed picture. Given the way the brain is hooked to the hands, his right hand, of course, will select a picture based on the scene flashed to his left hemisphere, and his left hand will select a picture based on the scene flashed to his right hemisphere. In this setup, one patient used his left hand (right hemisphere) to select a shovel to go with the snowy scene that his right hemisphere had seen, and his right hand (left hemisphere) to select a chicken's head to match the chicken's claw that his left hemisphere had seen. All so far is as we would expect.

When asked, however, to explain these choices, the patient's verbally more fluent (left) hemisphere responded as follows: "That's easy; the chicken claw goes with the chicken; and you need a shovel to clean out the chicken shed." The response of the left hemisphere makes sense of the left-hand action (which in reality indicates the intentions of the right hemisphere) *in its own terms*, using the resources available to it (what the left hemisphere has seen, namely, just a chicken claw). The response is unstrained and coherent. What the right hemisphere has seen and what caused it to pick out the shovel (the picture of the snowy scene) plays no role in the explanation, since the left hemisphere is unaware of it. And, significantly, the left hemisphere is "unbothered" (seemingly unaware) that it has no idea "really" why the left hand is holding a picture of a shovel.

This patient understood the surgery he had had, and he understood that his hemispheres were disconnected and could act independently of each other—or perhaps we ought to say that his left hemisphere and maybe also his right one understood these things. But note that the left hemisphere does not respond by saying that what the left hand (right hemisphere) does is not its responsibility, or that the right hemisphere controls the left hand, or, most significantly, that it does not know why in the world the left hand (right hemisphere) reached out for the shovel. The left hemisphere responds as though the motivating factors for the left hand's (right hemisphere–caused) action were its own, and not, in fact, the right hemisphere's (as they were).

What is striking, therefore, is that given its conscious understanding of the surgery and its implications, the left hemisphere of the patient does not explain the actions of the left hand as something the right brain did. This, indeed, might be the patient's view of the matter if he were sitting around being philosophical about his surgery or studying neurobiology. But even when just reminded of the right hemisphere's ability, the left hemisphere persists in explaining the action as if the action were something it had intended all along. In this case—and many others like it—the left hemisphere integrates the actions initiated by the right hemisphere into its own scheme of things.

Other split-brain patients show the same urge to ignore paradoxes and "make up" a coherent explanation (Gazzaniga 1983, 1985). It is as though the theoretical framework the brain uses to makes sense of its world will not tolerate or accommodate certain kinds of paradoxical, incoherent, or aberrant data. The left hemisphere is unwilling to entertain the hypothesis that parts of its own body act outside its intentions. Such a hypothesis is, in all likelihood, consistently rejected by healthy brains as well. Making sense of the world is as basic a function as anything the brain does. Moreover, as P. S. Churchland (1986) comments, evidence is accumulating, from a variety of different types of research, that even in people with normal brains, explanations of choices, moods, judgments, and so forth are less introspection driven than they are folk theory–driven (Allman, 1989; Cialdini, 1984; Nisbett and Ross, 1980).

The sort of phenomenon we have observed above with a particular split-brain patient has been observed hundreds of times on other such patients. When a simple command such as "walk" is flashed to the mute right hemisphere of a split-brain patient, the patient will typically respond by pushing his or her chair back and starting to leave the testing area. When asked where he or she is going, a typical response is "Going into my house to get a Coke" (Gazzaniga, 1985). As before, the left hemisphere is faced with the task of explaining an overt behavior that was initiated not by that hemisphere but by the disconnected right hemisphere.

MODULES OF THE MIND

I want to argue that this data from split-brain patients can give us insight into normal brain organization. A variety of neurobiologists and cognitive scientists, using a variety of theoretical and research paradigms, have argued recently that the normal brain is organized into different *modules* or subsystems (Atran, 1990; Chomsky, 1986; Fodor, 1983; Gardner, 1983; Garfield, 1987; Gazzaniga, 1985, 1988; Jackendoff, 1987). There may be hundreds or maybe even thousands of these modules, which themselves are organized into bigger systems (for example, grammar, musical abilities, orientation in space, common sense, and so on). These modules express themselves through forming expectations in the mind, emotions in the mind/body, or directing overt actions of the body; most of them, however, cannot express their workings through verbal communication. Most of these modules, like those existing in animals, can store information about experienced events, store affective reactions to those events, and respond to stimuli associated with a particular experience. These activities proceed with abandon without language.

The brain appears to be organized in such a way that information is stored and processed by these many different modules, modules which can compute, remember, feel emotion, and act. These modules pass on their computations (expectations, decisions, emotions, directions for action, and so on) to other modules, modules which can use language and which specialize in *interpretation*. These language and interpretive modules I will call (following Gazzaniga, 1985, 1988) *the interpreter*.

The interpreter use the "results" of the computations of the other, nonlinguistic, modules, but has no real access to how these results were reached. The internal workings of these other modules are "encapsulated," "sealed off" from consciousness and from language. Only their "decisions" or "results" are passed on. This type of brain organization seems to be necessary if humans (or other animals) are to act quickly and efficiently in the world for survival, though it does not necessarily give rise to "true" interpretations of our behaviors.[2]

The modularity of the mind, and the encapsulation of these modules, is easy to demonstrate also with "normal" subjects in regard to everyday behaviors. People are quite able to judge whether a sentence of their language is grammatical or not (say, the grammatical sentences "The South Pole is uninhabited" and "The South Pole is inhabited by Eskimos" versus the ungrammatical sentence "The South Pole is uninhabited by Eskimos"), but they have no access whatsoever to the computations by which they reached such decisions. People can say whether two sentences have the same meaning (for example, compare "Children are easy to please" and "It is easy to please children," which have the same meaning, with "Children are eager to please" and "It is eager to please children," which do not). Once again, people appear to have no real insight into (and cannot coherently say) how they reached such judgments. When they do give reasons, these reasons are almost always clearly "wrong" from any linguistic perspective (Radford, 1990).

Likewise, people can recognize the face of a given individual across varying ages and conditions of health. They cannot, however, say how they have done this, and scientists still have only the poorest understanding of this remarkable ability in human beings. Finally, we can note that people can often say how they feel emotionally, but that psychotherapy thrives on the fact that they often cannot accurately say why, or at least, they are prone to accept a rather wide range of views as to why they feel as they do (Ortony, Clore, & Collins, 1988).

THE INTERPRETER

There appear to be unique neural systems present in the left hemisphere of (right-handed) humans that compel the brain to make sense out of the diverse behaviors humans produce. I have called these systems (following Gazzaniga) the brain's *interpreter*. The interpreter specializes in making inferences and constructing explanations, based on the decisions and results of the other modules in the mind and their processing of our experience of the outside world and of our own emotions; that is, it specializes in forming beliefs and constructing "theories." The interpreter is intimately connected to a person's developing "beliefs" about the nature of the self, and is the source of all of our "folk theories." With its evolutionary appearance in our species, we humans were freed from the tedious processes of learning only by trial and error.

A brain system that can make inferences about events in the real world must also make inferences about its own behaviors. Once beliefs and theories were in place, thanks to the interpreter, the human organism no longer lived only in the present. As Michael Gazzaniga (1985, 99) puts it: "The montage of conditioned responses that had governed biological creatures for all of time now dwelt in a brain system capable of thwarting their power." The interpreter calls upon a large number of separate and relatively independent modules for its information, modules whose internal workings the interpreter is not privy to.

Gazzaniga gives a couple of interesting examples of the everyday workings of the interpreter: You feel cheerful and content visiting with friends at home on Monday evening. But on waking on Tuesday morning, your mood has darkened for no apparent reason. You wonder what has happened. Your actual data about your life have not changed over night. Why has your mood changed, then? Gazzaniga argues that a nonverbal module has somehow been activated, and the emotional associates of the events stored in that module have been communicated to the brain's emotional system. Humans are constantly being conditioned to have particular emotional responses, and the particular modules in the brain that store that information can become activated for expression by any of a number of means. Something in your sleep or in your morning experiences has triggered the emotional associations of the contents of some module. You don't know what or why. In this particular case of the Tuesday morning blues, a negative mood is felt. If you let the process stop there, life would be simpler. But you begin to interpret previously neutral, negative, or even positive events more negatively as a result of having to explain this new mood.

This example deals with the subtle manipulations of mood and how they interact to change one's beliefs about things, people, and events. But the same thing can happen in regard to overt behaviors. Consider another of Gazzaniga's examples (which I elaborate in a somewhat different direction than Gazzaniga, perhaps): a happily married man who believes in fidelity goes along to the annual Christmas party and after too much to drink winds up in bed next to a woman who is not his wife.

He is participating in a behavior that is at odds with his beliefs about marriage and fidelity. What may happen, of course, is that he changes his evaluation of the importance of fidelity to marriage. Seeing his own behavior and unable to live in a state of cognitive dissonance between his belief in marriage and fidelity and this actual behavior he has engaged in, he "explains" his behavior by claiming to himself that he doesn't really believe in fidelity but that at a "deeper" level he needs to freely express himself through the exploration of other women. His belief in fidelity was just the result of the "rut" he was in, and so on, and so forth, through the intricacies of a theory that is but a "post hoc" explanation of his own mood and behavior, the causes of which he is not privy to. And we might note that many of those who would claim that this man does have, or could have, some "privileged" access to his own motives and the causes of his behavior are those who want to charge him a hefty fee to help him gain "access" to it.

SELF-DECEPTION AND THE INTERPRETER

I have mentioned above that it may well be that the human brain is organized the way it is because it is a system that gives rise to efficient and fast action. If we had to (or were tempted to) look into every nook and cranny of the workings of our minds before carrying out decisions, we would never act (Langer, 1989). Acting on generalizations that are not completely correct is often more efficient that pure trial and error, even if sometimes we are wrong and pay for it. However, there may be a yet deeper reason that the human interpreter works the way it does, spinning out "coherent" and "facile" explanations, even when it has little access to crucial information locked away in the internal, but encapsulated workings of its mind. This "deeper" reason lies in the origins of primate, and human, intelligence.

There has been, for some time now, a debate in primatology as to why chimpanzees and gorillas are so intelligent. After all, their lives are rather easy, and the environmental conditions of their lives do not appear to demand anything like the intelligence they actually have (Goodall, 1986). They have no natural predators other than humans, who have only recently played a big role in wiping out the environments of these primates (and, despite popular myths to the contrary, our prehistoric human ancestors probably never hunted and ate "lower" primates in any significant numbers, Binford, 1981, 1983, 1987). Furthermore, to eat, they have only to reach out and grab a handful of leaves (or, in the case of chimpanzees, occasionally reach out and grab a helpless baby baboon).

If intelligence evolved in response to environmental pressure, as any other significant biological function, why did so environmentally unchallenged a creature as a chimpanzee or a gorilla end up so intelligent? Lots of theories have been put forward about the matter, one of which is currently leading to something of a new paradigm in the study of human intelligence. In Donald Johanson and James Shreeve's recent book, *Lucy's Child: The Discovery of a Human Ancestor* (1989), Johanson surveys the argument that *society* itself was the driving force behind primate intelligence and the eventual development of specifically human intelligence. Much of my discussion below is based on Johanson and Shreeve's book.

Society drives the development of intelligence in several ways. The development of social groups allows for the young of the group to *learn* from others crucial information about the nature of the environment the group lives in and ways to deal with it. Chimpanzees, for instance, do not come into the world knowing how to fashion a twig into a probe that can be used to fish termites from their nest; nor would all of them hit on it if left to their own devices. Most of them learn to use twigs to fish termites by watching older, more experienced members of their group (Goodall, 1986). Learning means that crucial information need not be stored innately in the genes nor discovered by trial and error by each individual separately.

Group living and learning stems from and allows for *cooperative behavior*. Such behavior allows the group to achieve what no individual working alone could accomplish, or at least as easily accomplish. A group of lions or chimpanzees can hunt more effectively as a group than as individuals. And they are all the better if they are able to pass down to their young, through learning, tricks of the trade. Social groups would become increasingly complex and cooperative as new environmental pressures added to the usefulness of intelligence.

But this sort of intelligence linked to learning and cooperative behavior gives rise, in the context of the dictates of the process of evolution, to something of a paradox. Though the members of a social group behave cooperatively, especially toward close kin, every individual is out to ensure the survival of his or her own genes (Dawkins, 1976, 1987). Each individual will be competing *within the group* for pieces of the resource pie, such as chances to mate and opportunities to feed.

It is well known (Dawkins, 1987; Douglas, 1986), both in evolutionary theory and in political theory, that, in a group, an individual acting only on his own self-interest, but taking advantage of the cooperative behaviors of the group, will always "outcompete" ("outsurvive") individuals acting only in the whole group's interest, unless there are sanctions against such an individual. There will always be a temptation for individuals to pursue their own self-interest by "outwitting" other members of the group through taking advantage of others' cooperative behaviors. And individuals so tempted will flourish if they indeed do "outwit" the others in the group. However, it takes a different sort of intelligence to outwit an intelligent adversary who is simultaneously trying to outwit *you*, an intelligence of a different order than it takes to "outwit" some termites out of reach in the ground, or to fool a helpless baby gazelle.

What we see here is that self-interest within the framework of cooperative groups will give rise to what some primatologists call "Machiavellian intelligence." This view of social intelligence places great emphasis on the *political* advantages of being smart. Cunning and calculation certainly do not exhaust the cognitive repertoire of chimpanzees and gorillas. Nevertheless, according to these primatologists, what matters in a social group is not so much *what* you know but *whom* you know, as well as how effective you can be at keeping critical knowledge out of the hands of those who might oppose you.

Primatologists used to believe that a physically weaker member of a group was doomed to submission on the bottom of a dominance hierarchy. But recent observations of baboon, monkey, and chimp interactions in the wild show this is not the case. The physically weaker individual can recruit stronger allies who can be depended upon to come to its aid when needed. These alliances are very often formed between kin: for example, a young rhesus macaque quickly discovers that she can intimidate far larger members of her group because her high-ranking mother will always back her up in any conflict. She eventually comes to occupy a place in the female hierarchy just below her mother.

Looked at in this way, the most basic kind of social intelligence is the ability to understand and remember the web of kin relationships that form the basis of a social group. However, human groups characteristically grow beyond mere "kin groups"—indeed, this is a prerequisite for larger human communities, cities, and states. And, crucially, primatologists are discovering political alliances among *unrelated* individuals in primate groups, individuals who share no genetic inheritance that might otherwise explain their favored treatment of each other.

To take one example of a great (and growing) many: primatologist Meredith Small of Cornell University recently reported the case of a low-ranking Barbary macaque (named Becky) in a captive community in southern France (Small, 1989, cited in Johanson & Shreeve, 1989). Over a period of months, Becky judiciously groomed and cared for the infants of females well above her in rank. Through these behaviors she managed to defy the normally rigid female hierarchy in macaques and advanced several rungs on the social ladder. To accomplish this feat, Becky had to know who was powerful enough to merit time spent gaining their favor and, more importantly, she had to have some conception of a "payoff" weeks, even months, down the road. Becky was, indeed, a very smart macaque. She and her genes were going places.

There are now a great many such examples from all over the primate world. But forming alliances is only the beginning. If it takes intelligence for a baboon or monkey to keep track of all the social relationships in her group, imagine how much intelligence is required when she and her companions begin to lie. And "telling lies" is, indeed, also commonly reported across the primate world. For example, consider the case of a juvenile chacma baboon named Paul observed in Ethiopia by Richard Byrne and Andrew Whiten (1987, cited in Johanson & Shreeve, 1989; see also Byrne & Whiten, 1988).

One day, Paul was watching an adult female named Mel digging in the ground for a large grass root. Paul looked around. There were no other baboons nearby, though the troop was well within earshot. Suddenly, with no visible provocation, Paul let out a yell. His mother quickly came on the scene and chased the astonished Mel out of sight, while Paul walked over and ate the grass root Mel had left behind. Paul had misled his mother into believing that he was being attacked, when in fact he was not. Paul pulled the same trick several times on other unsuspecting adults.

Many other such examples have been reported for other primates. One researcher (example cited in Johanson & Shreeve, 1989, 275) reported watching a female hamadryas baboon slowly shuffle over toward a large rock, pretending all the while to forage while keeping an eye on the harem male in the group. After twenty minutes she ended up with her head and shoulders visible to the big male, but her hands engaged in the illicit activity of grooming a favorite subordinate male, who was hidden from view behind the rock. In this case, and the others like it, the deceiver is engaged in a prodigious mental performance. She has set upon a course of action based not only on what she *knows* about her social milieu—who is strong, who is weak, who is most likely to help—but also on what she *imagines* to be going on inside another animal's head.

Richard Alexander (1971, 1989) has applied these sorts of ideas directly to human origins (see also Goodall, 1986, 530–34 and Johanson & Shreeve, 1989, 275–80). Only we humans have achieved "ecological dominance" by eliminating whatever threat the environment might pose to our survival. The forces of natural selection no longer act upon us with the force they do in the case of other animals, and they have not done so for some time. What drives human evolution now is not natural selection through disease and environmental change, but the evolution of the brain and human intelligence.

Alexander (1989) argued that the human mind is the product of a runaway intellect fueled by intense conflicts of interest both within and between groups. Though groups may harbor much internal conflict based on self-interest and competition among members of the group, any social group whose members cooperated more effectively than the members of other groups would have a genetic advantage over those other groups whose members were less adept at getting along for a common purpose. A "balance of power race" between groups would emerge, each forced to evolve ever-finer cooperative skills and to stress more and more their "in-group," "us versus them" mentality, simply to keep from being outcompeted or even annihilated by neighboring groups trapped in the same evolutionary spiral.

Alexander places a high premium on the social skills of manipulation and deceit. In fact, he argues, plausibly, I believe, that there would be no need for a thinking organ as powerful as the human mind in a universe where everyone told the truth. If there is an advantage to deception, both for individuals within a group in their intragroup competition and for groups as a whole in their intergroup competition with other groups, then the best deceivers would be those skilled in *self-deception*. No deception is so successful as the one in which even the deceiver is unaware of his own ulterior motives. He thus avoids the risk of betraying them and himself.

Self-deception would carry a powerful advantage particularly in intergroup conflicts, especially as groups became ever larger. The members of small social units would be predisposed to cooperative behavior simply because they are closely related to each other. If my kin survive, even if I die, some significant portion of my genetic inheritance survives. But this is not so for non-kin, even if they are members of my social group. As group size grew, the *us* in "us versus them"—the members of one's own group, whether clansmen, fellow residents in a city, or countrymen— would no longer be close kin and might in fact be no more closely related to each other genetically than members of rival groups. Any self-deception that would promote group unity under such circumstances would give the group a selective advantage in its conflicts with other groups by making it more cooperative. These self-deceptions could be binding beliefs in tribal ritual or myth, in an organized religion, in patriotism, or in a particular political "ideology."

If self-deception, that is, believing in "satisfying accounts" that underwrite one's self- or group interest, are the evolutionary basis of our runaway intelligence and ecological dominance as a species, then the organization of the brain we argued for above makes a great deal of sense. The brain efficiently computes decisions, moods, and actions with hundreds of speedy and encapsulated modules. The interpreter needs no access to the internal workings of these modules—which would just slow it and them down in any case—since its job is in reality to tell the "best story" it can, not to give an "accurate" account of the workings of the world or its own mind. And the best account is liable to be one that "satisfies" the self- and group interest of the individual.

The interpreter is far more "attuned" to viewpoints embedded in the individual's social groups and their practices than it is to "truth" in any sense that resides outside these groups and their practices. If it were not so, Paul would have gone without Mel's grass root, and we without our tales that breathing poison air in Los Angeles and other major cities is "progress" or that the "evil empire" of the Soviet Union was an everlasting, implacable foe, meriting the expenditure of billions of dollars on weapons rather than on homeless people.

CONCLUSION

I have argued in this chapter that the human brain has in it hundreds or thousands of modules or subsystems storing and processing a myriad of associations (for example, among features of birds and their habitats) based on our experiences in the world. It has in it also other systems (which are capable of using language) that *interpret* experience and the results of the workings of its many modules. I called these systems the "interpreter." The interpreter forms "folk theories," which together with the nonlinguistic modules of the mind, cause the person to talk and act in certain ways (for instances, go look for birds in a given area or report a memory in a certain way at a certain time).

The various social groups to which one belongs engage in various social practices that I have called "Discourses." Discourses are amalgams of ways of talking, valuing, thinking, believing, interacting, acting, and, sometimes, writing and reading, together with various "props" (books, clubs, buildings, birds, and so on) in the world. Discourses are tied to particular social groups and the "identities" their members take on when playing their apportioned "roles" within the social practices of the group.

Discourses *apprentice* new members to ensure that they lay down in their modules some crucially relevant associations and that they form appropriate folk theories—that is, that their interpreters find certain ways of making sense appropriate and satisfying. They also continue to "discipline" the associations and folk theories of members of the group, ensuring that they stay "close enough" to the norms of the group to allow for cooperative behavior and the survival of the group.

What is in the heads of the members of the group is less important than the "ideal" or "normative" associations and folk theories embedded in the group practice, toward which everyone converges, more or less. This "ideal norm" is not in anyone's head, but embedded in the history and social practices of the group. It is discoverable by "thick description" (Geertz, 1973) of the group and its history and practices, a species of ethnography. I take psychology to be the study of mind/brains with their modules (associations) and interpreters (folk theories) in the context of such thick descriptions of the Discourses of socially defined groups. Much of what the psychologist ought to study, in this view, is not in a laboratory and not in anyone's head.

Finally, I have argued that given the way in which the interpreter is organized in relation to the mind/brain as a whole, and considering how it arose in the evolution of human intelligence, *we ought not to trust* that it will give rise to veridical accounts of the physical or social world, or to a humane organization of human society. Of course, this raises the issue of how we could ever gain a "veridical" account of the physical or social world (whatever this might mean) or argue for a given ethical basis for human society. That is an issue we must leave for later. Clearly, it would necessitate a consideration of the history and philosophy of science, on the one hand, and of ethical systems that demand the consideration of other people's points of view, and not just our own or our own group's, on the other (see Chapter 1 of Gee, 1990c, for some discussion of such an ethical system).

But there is one crucial thing a human can do, and which Paul the baboon cannot. Humans can pretend to be someone else, and from the pretence of someone else's interpreter feel damaged, cheated, or angered by their "real" selves. This ability—which is in all likelihood a rather accidental evolutionary epiphenomena of our ability to manipulate and deceive, and which is not all that commonly practiced—is, I would argue, one of the crucial bases of the human ability, however tenuous and tentative, to think, imagine, and sometimes act beyond our own interpreters.

NOTES

1. On my use of the terms "cultural model" and "folk theory," see chap. 1, n. 2.

2. For a somewhat different interpretation of Gazzaniga's work, see Bickerton, 1990, Chapter 8. In this chapter Bickerton discusses much of the material I survey in this section, the previous one, and the next. Despite differences in emphases, I consider Bickerton's fascinating book to give further and extended support for the conclusions I am arguing for in this chapter, though Bickerton might not agree with my reading of his book.

5

SOCIETY

DISCOURSES

In the preceding chapters I have linked the workings of the mind/brain
to social practices which I have called "Discourses" (Gee 1989a, 1990c).
Each Discourse in a society is "owned" and "operated" by a socioculturally defined group of people. These people are accepted as "members"
of the Discourse and play various "roles," give various "performances,"
within it. Each Discourse involves ways of talking, acting, interacting,
valuing, and believing, as well as the spaces and material "props" the
group uses to carry out its social practices. Discourses integrate words,
acts, values, beliefs, attitudes, social identities, as well as gestures,
glances, body positions, and clothes.

Discourses are always ways of displaying (through words, actions, values,
and beliefs) *membership* in a particular social group or social network (people
who associate with each other around a common set of interests, goals, and
activities). Being trained (apprenticed) as a linguist meant that I learned to
speak, think, and act like a linguist and to recognize others when they do so
(not just that I learned lots of facts about language and linguistics). So "being
a linguist" is one of the Discourses I have mastered.

Actually, matters are not that simple: the larger Discourse of linguistics
contains many sub-Discourses, different socially accepted ways of being
a linguist. But the master Discourse is not just the sum of its parts, it is
something also over and above them. Every act of speaking, writing, and
behaving that a linguist does as a linguist is meaningful only against the

background of the whole social institution of linguistics, and that institution is made up of concrete things like people, books, and buildings; abstract things like bodies of knowledge, values, norms, and beliefs; mixtures of concrete and abstract things like universities, journals, and publishers; and shared history and shared stories.

There are innumerable Discourses in any modern, technological, urban-based society: for example, (enacting) being (a type of) an American or an Afro-American, a man or a woman, a member of a certain socioeconomic class, a factory worker or an executive, a doctor or a hospital patient, a teacher, an administrator, or a student, a student of physics or of literature, a member of a club or a street gang, or a regular at the local bar. Discourses are always embedded in a medley of social institutions and often involve various "props" like books and magazines of various sorts, laboratories, classrooms, buildings of various sorts, various technologies, and a myriad of other objects from sewing needles (for sewing circles) through birds (for bird-watchers) to basketball courts and basketballs (for basketball players).

Discourses ensure that their members (1) get apprenticed; (2) gain similar associative links in their mental networks, similar enough for the practice to continue; and (3) pick up folk theories common to the group. The Discourse "disciplines" people's networks and folk theories so as to keep them "in line." If people's networks or folk theory get too "deviant," the Discourse ensures that they have experiences that bring their networks and/or folk theories back toward the "norm," or that they leave the practice. The Discourse rewards and sanctions characteristic ways of acting, talking, believing, valuing, and interacting, and in doing so it incorporates a normative or ideal set of mental associations and folk theories, toward which its members more or less converge. These norms, discoverable by ethnographic study, are, in fact, where the *meanings* of the acts, beliefs, values, and words of the group reside.

There are multiple and complex relationships among Discourses, individuals, and their actions. We can distinguish between "primary Discourses" and "secondary Discourses" (the following discussion is based, in part, on my 1990 book *Social Linguistics and Literacies: Ideologies in Discourses*). Primary Discourses are Discourses to which people are apprenticed early in life during their primary socialization as members of particular families within their sociocultural settings. They are our first social identity, a base within which we acquire or resist later Discourses. Secondary Discourses are Discourses to which people are apprenticed as part of their socializations within various local, state, and national groups and institutions outside early home and peer-group socialization—for example, churches, gangs, schools, offices.

Our primary Discourse establishes those people who count as "people like us" in our private and informal lives. Our primary Discourse, which always effects behaviors in secondary Discourses to a certain extent, is like a theme that runs through all of our behaviors (sometimes very submerged, sometimes quite apparent). It constitutes our *personal persona* and is part of what gives a sense of unity and identity to our multiple social selves (constituted by our many secondary Discourses). Many complicated things can happen in the case of primary Discourses. For example, certain social circumstances can lead to an individual not having (much) of one, or having several of them (sometimes conflicting), or disowning "people like us (me)" and engaging in various degrees of self-hatred.

As we enter the "public" world beyond our families and kin group, we take on new identities as members of various secondary Discourses, from school- and community-based Discourses through a large number of later ones (for example, the army, business, fraternities, job sites, professions, and the like). Each secondary Discourse is a tradition passed down through time—ways people who "belong" to the Discourse tend to behave now and have behaved in the past in certain settings. This tradition constrains what can happen in the present, since only what is similar enough to what has happened in the past will be recognizable as a meaningful performance in the Discourse. Yet, at the same time, actual acts (performances) constitute the ever-growing and changing history of the Discourse. Each performance must be similar enough to earlier ones to get recognized, but each has the capacity to be just "new" enough to also change what counts as a recognizable performance in the future.

It is an interesting fact about the human condition that we can actually be members of two conflicting Discourses, thus living out internally and in the world the opposition between our Discourses. This happens to nearly everyone at some level, but is, of course, particularly acute, for example, in the case of many urban black teenagers who want to be members of "street culture" (which uses resistance to the school as a sign of membership) and still succeed in school (Erickson, 1987; Hewitt, 1986; McDermott, 1987a, b; Ogbu, 1978, 1983, 1987; Trueba, 1989). And, of course, there are deep conflicts between many minority home-based primary Discourses and various dominant Discourses in the schools and the society at large, which are often controlled in the interest of elites who are reluctant to truly share power with minorities.

Any human action is meaningful and recognizable only within some Discourse. Secondary Discourses are the Discourses we belong to thanks to our "public" apprenticeships in Discourses beyond the home and family, rooted in the "public" world of the community, state, or nation. They constitute the recognizability and meaningfulness of our "public" (more formal) acts. A particular woman, for instance, might be recognized as a *businesswoman, political activist, feminist, church member, National Organization of Women official, PTA member, teacher's aide, volunteer Planned Parenthood counselor*, and many more, by carrying out performances that are recognizable within and by these Discourses.

Primary Discourses and secondary Discourses are related. We saw above in Chapter 1, in the discussion of the five-year-old's birthday-party story, that behaviors (ways of talking, acting, thinking, valuing, and so on) can *filter* or drift from various secondary Discourses (for example, various school-based Discourses) into the home-based practices of primary Discourses. Thus, many mainstream, middle-class homes incorporate some school-based (secondary Discourse) practices into their dinnertime talk or "book-reading" episodes with their children. On the other hand, behaviors from primary Discourses can also *filter* or drift from primary Discourses into various secondary Discourses. Schools have adopted many values, attitudes, and ways of behaving (having little actually to do with education) from middle-class homes (Cazden, 1988; Gee, 1990c; Heath, 1983). Black churches have been deeply influenced by black primary Discourses and have in turn influenced them (Davis, 1985; Smitherman, 1977; Stuckey, 1987).

It makes equal sense to say that an act belongs to an individual and that it belongs to a Discourse. People act, but since it is Discourses that render their acts meaningful and recognizable, it is also Discourses that act (Clifford, 1988; Douglas, 1986; Eagleton, 1984; Fleck, 1979; Foucault, 1972, 1973, 1977, 1980, 1985; Giddens, 1984; H. J. Graff, 1987; Holton, 1988; Luke, 1988; White, 1973). A person's different acts are rendered recognizable by a variety of different and sometimes conflicting Discourses, and thus, the individual is not really a unified creature, but rather the center (agent/actor) of varied, and sometimes conflicting, acts (performances).

Of course, most of us tell ourselves we are unified wholes, but even this telling will vary, depending upon the secondary or primary Discourse (or mixture thereof) out of which we attempt it each time we "renew" our story of ourselves (Connerton, 1989; Middleton & Edwards, 1990). Thus, even our "story" about who we are is a performance that varies with the stage on which we carry it out.

This Discourse-based theory allows room for both individual *creativity* and for social *resistance* to domination and hegemony (see Callinicos, 1988, for an interesting discussion of these issues). Creativity is allowed both by the fact that every act can vary just so long as it still "counts" as within the Discourse and by the fact that one can balance roles that actually simultaneously "count" in two or more Discourses and in the act of this admixture create rather "novel" performances. Both of these can change Discourses and even lead to new ones: the "style" with which I carry out a recognizable act "catches on" with others; or the simultaneous balancing/mixing of several roles begins to count as the single role in a new emergent Discourse.

Possible change in Discourses and the emergence of new ones can open up possibilities for resistance to domination and hegemony. For example, a person from a dominated primary Discourse (say an urban, lower-socioeconomic black person), if she is allowed access to a dominant secondary Discourse, can "pull off" performances with enough influence from her dominated primary Discourse so as to eventually widen what counts as an acceptable performance (and thus an acceptable person) in the dominant Discourse. Of course, only people who get access can do this and only people able and willing to live with the initial cognitive dissonance and conflicts. Such people are one of the leading edges of resistance and change.

Furthermore, one Discourse can always openly oppose another one. Such open warfare does not always end in the victory of the dominant Discourse. Since Discourses can't exist unless their sanctioned roles and performances get acted out by individuals, to the extent that these roles and performances are frustrated, the Discourse, no matter how dominant, is endangered.

This discussion has reviewed a number of important points that one can make about Discourses (Belsey, 1980; Eagleton, 1983; Gee, 1987; Jameson, 1981; Macdonell, 1986; Thompson, 1984). I have summarized them in the list below:

1. Discourses are inherently "ideological." They crucially involve a set of values and viewpoints about the social and political (power) relationships between people and the distribution of social goods (at the very least about who is an insider and who isn't, but often many others as well). One must speak and act and at least appear to think and feel in terms of these values and viewpoints while being in the Discourse; otherwise one doesn't count as being in it.

2. Discourses are resistant to internal criticism and self-scrutiny since uttering viewpoints that seriously undermine them defines one as being outside them. The Discourse itself defines what counts as acceptable criticism. Of course, one can criticize a particular Discourse from the viewpoint of another one (for example, psychology criticizing linguistics). But what one cannot do is stand outside all Discourses and criticize any or all of them. Criticism must always be lodged from some set of assumed values, attitudes, beliefs, and ways of talking/writing and, thus, from within some Discourse.

3. Discourse-defined positions from which to speak and behave are not, however, just defined internal to a Discourse, but also as standpoints taken up by the Discourse in its relation to other, ultimately opposing, Discourses. The Discourse of managers in an industry is partly defined as a set of views, norms, and standpoints defined by their opposition to analogous points in the Discourse of workers (Macdonell, 1986, 1–7). The Discourse we identify with being a feminist is radically changed if all male Discourses disappear. The Discourse of a regular drinking group at a bar is partly defined by its points of opposition to a variety of other viewpoints (nondrinkers, people who dislike bars as places of meeting people, Yuppies, and so forth).

4. Any Discourse concerns itself with certain objects and puts forward certain concepts, viewpoints, and values at the expense of others. In doing so it will *marginalize* viewpoints and values central to other Discourses (Macdonell, 1986, 1–7). In fact, a Discourse can call for one to accept values in conflict with other Discourses of which one is also a member. For example, the Discourse used in literature departments used to marginalize popular literature and women's writings (though times are changing in this regard). Further, women readers of Hemingway, for instance, when acting as "acceptable readers" by the standards of the Discourse of traditional literary criticism might find themselves complicit with values which conflicted with the values of various other Discourses they belonged to as women (for example, various feminist Discourses; see Culler, 1982, 43–64; Greene & Kahn, 1985; Toril, 1985; Todd, 1988).

5. Finally, Discourses are intimately related to the distribution of social power and hierarchical structure in society (this is why they are always and everywhere ideological; see point 1). Control over certain Discourses can lead to the acquisition of social goods (money, power, status) in a society (for example, the Discourse of successful "mainstream," middle-class job interviewing, in which one takes an overly optimistic view of one's abilities and role-plays confidence one doesn't have, and which many minorities and women have not mastered). These Discourses empower those groups who have the fewest or most minor conflicts with their other Discourses when they use them. For

example, many academic, legalistic, and bureaucratic Discourses in our society contain a moral sub-Discourse that sees "right" as what is derivable from general abstract principles. This can conflict to a degree with a Discourse about morality that appears to be more often associated with women than men in terms of which "wrong" is seen as the disruption of social networks, and "right" as the repair of those networks (Belenky, Clinchy, Goldberger, & Tarule, 1986; Gilligan, 1982, 1986). Or, to take another example, the Discourse of traditional literary criticism used to be a standard route to success as a professor of literature. Since it conflicted less with the other Discourses of white, middle-class men than it did with those of women, men were empowered by it. Women were not, as they were often at cross-purposes when engaging in it.

ACQUISITION VERSUS LEARNING

How do people come by the Discourses they are members of? Here it is necessary, before answering the question, to make an important distinction, a distinction that does not exist in nontechnical parlance: a distinction between *acquisition* and *learning*.[1] I will distinguish these two as follows:

Acquisition is a process of acquiring something subconsciously by exposure to models, a process of trial and error, and practice within social groups, without formal teaching. It happens in natural settings that are meaningful and functional in the sense that acquirers know that they need to acquire the thing they are exposed to in order to function and that they in fact want to so function. This is how most people come to control their first language.

Learning is a process that involves conscious knowledge gained through teaching (though not necessarily from someone officially designated a teacher) or through certain life experiences that trigger conscious reflection. This teaching or reflection involves explanation and analysis, that is, breaking down the thing to be learned into its analytic parts. It inherently involves attaining, along with the matter being taught, some degree of metaknowledge about the matter.

Much of what we come by in life, after our initial enculturation, involves a mixture of acquisition and learning. However, the balance between the two can be quite different in different cases and different at different stages in the developmental process. For instance, I initially learned to drive a car by instruction, but thereafter acquired, rather than learned, most of what I know.

Some cultures highly value acquisition and so tend simply to expose children to adults modeling some activity; eventually the child picks it up, as a gestalt rather than as a series of analytic bits (Heath, 1983; Scollon & Scollon, 1981; Street, 1984). Other cultural groups highly value teaching and thus break down what is to be mastered into sequential steps and analytic parts and engage in explicit explanation.

Both acquisition and learning have an up side and a downside that can be expressed as follows: we are better at performing what we acquire, but we consciously know more about what we have learned. For most of us, playing a musical instrument or dancing or using a second language are skills we attained by some mixture of acquisition and learning. But it is a safe bet that, over the same amount of time, people are better at (performing) these activities if acquisition predominated during that time.

The point can be made using second language as the example: most people aren't very good at attaining a second language in any very functional way through formal instruction in a classroom. That's why teaching grammar is not a very good way of getting people to control a language. However, people who have acquired a second language in a natural setting don't thereby make good linguists, and some good linguists can't speak the languages they learned in a classroom.

What is said here about second languages is true, I believe, of all Discourses: acquisition is good for performance, learning is good for metalevel knowledge. Acquisition and learning are thus, too, differential sources of power: acquirers usually beat learners at performance, whereas learners usually beat acquirers at talking about it—that is, at explication, explanation, analysis, and criticism.

What has been argued, controversially, to be true in the case of second-language development is, I would argue, much less controversially true of Discourses: Discourses are mastered through *acquisition*, not *learning*. That is, Discourses are not mastered by overt instruction (even less so than languages, and hardly anyone ever fluently acquired a second language sitting in a classroom), but by enculturation ("apprenticeship") into social practices through scaffolded and supported interaction with people who have already mastered the Discourse (Newman, Griffin, & Cole, 1989; Tharp & Gallimore, 1988). This is how we all acquired our native language and our home-based Discourse. It is how we acquire all later, more public-oriented Discourses. If you have no access to the social practice, you don't get in the Discourse, you don't have it.

As a Discourse is being mastered (or after it has been) by acquisition, then, of course, learning can facilitate "metaknowledge," but learning can facilitate nothing unless the acquisition process has already begun. You cannot overtly teach anyone a Discourse, in a classroom or anywhere else. This is not to say that acquisition can't go on in a classroom but only that if it does, this isn't because of overt "teaching," but because of a process of "apprenticeship" and social practice. Acquisition must (at least, partially) precede learning; apprenticeship must precede overt teaching. Classrooms that do not properly balance acquisition and learning, and realize which is which, and which student has acquired what, simply privilege those students who have begun the acquisition process at home, engaging these students in a teaching/learning process, while the others simply "fail."

It is very important to realize that the English language often leads us to confuse terms for products/props/content and terms for Discourses. Thus, take an academic discipline like linguistics. You can overtly teach someone (the content knowledge of the discipline of) *linguistics*, which is a body of facts and theories; however, while knowledge of some significant part of these facts and theories is necessary to actually being a linguist, you cannot overtly teach anyone *to be (to behave like) a linguist*, which is a Discourse—you can just let them practice being a linguist (apprentice them) with people who are already in the Discourse.

A person could know a great deal about linguistics and still not be (accepted as) a linguist (not able to signal membership in the "club" by the right type of talk, writing, values, attitudes, and behaviors). "Auto-didacts" are precisely people who, while often extremely knowledgeable, trained themselves and thus were trained outside a process of group practice and socialization. They are almost never accepted as "insiders," "members of the club (profession, group)." Our Western focus on individualism makes us constantly forget the importance of having been properly socialized.

Let me turn now to the proviso in the definition of learning above about "certain life experiences that trigger conscious reflection," causing the same effects as overt teaching. In my definition of learning, I am concerned with what usually or prototypically counts as "teaching" in our culture. This involves breaking down what is to be taught into its analytic bits and getting learners to learn it in such a way that they can "talk about," "describe," "explain" it. That is, the learner is meant to have "metaknowledge" about what is learned and to be able to engage in "metatalk" about it (what often goes under the name "critical thinking"). We often teach even things like driving this way. But not all cultures engage in this sort of teaching, and not all of them use the concept "teaching" in this way; nor, indeed, do all instances of what is sometimes called "teaching" in our own culture fit this characterization (Heath, 1983; Scribner & Cole, 1981; Scollon & Scollon, 1981; Street, 1984).

In many cultures where there is no such overt analytical teaching, some people still gain a good deal of "metaknowledge" about what they know and do. This appears to come about by that fact they have had certain experiences which have caused them to think about a particular Discourse in a reflective and critical way (Goody, 1977; 1986, 1–44). When we have really mastered anything (for example, a Discourse), we have little or no conscious awareness of it (indeed, like dancing, Discourses wouldn't work if people were consciously aware of what they were doing while doing it). However, when we come across a situation in which we are unable to accommodate or adapt, we become consciously aware of what we are trying to do or are being called upon to do (Vygotsky, 1987, 167–241). While such an experience can happen to anyone, they are common among people who are somewhat "marginal" to a Discourse or culture, and, thus, such people often have insights into the workings of these Discourses or cultures that more "mainstream" members do not. This is, in fact, the advantage to being "socially maladapted" (as long as the maladaptation is not too dysfunctional and, to be sure, this is not to say that there are not also disadvantages). And, of course, people in our culture can have such experiences apart from classrooms (and often have them *in* classrooms when it is the classroom, school, or teacher that is causing the maladaptation).

Let me give an example that works similarly, and which further illuminates the nature of learning via teaching or reflective life experiences: the case of classroom second-language learning. Almost no one really acquires a second language in a classroom. However, it can happen that exposure to another language, having to translate it into and otherwise relate it to your own language, can cause you to become consciously aware of how your first language works (how it means). This "metaknowledge" can actually make one better able to manipulate one's first language.

Vygotsky says that learning "a foreign language allows the child to understand his native language as a single instantiation of a linguistic system" (1987, 222). Ruth Finnegan (1988), in a study of the Limba, a nonliterate group in Sierra Leone, points out that the Limba have a great deal of metalinguistic and reflective sophistication in their talk about language, sophistication of the sort that we normally think is the product of writing and formal schooling, neither of which the Limba have. Finnegan attributes this sophistication to the Limba's multiple contacts with speakers of other languages and with those languages themselves.

And here we have a clue, then. Classroom instruction (in composition, study skills, writing, critical thinking, content-based literacy, or whatever) can lead to metaknowledge, to seeing how the Discourses you have already got relate to those you are attempting to acquire, and how those you are trying to acquire relate to self and society.

There is no doubt that many minority and lower socioeconomic students have great difficulty accommodating to or adapting to certain "mainstream" Discourses, in particular, many school-based Discourses. These Discourses often conflict seriously (in values, attitudes, ways of acting, thinking, and talking) with their own home- and community-based Discourses (Erickson, 1987; McDermott, 1987a, b; Rosaldo, 1989; Trueba, 1987, 1989). And, furthermore, these mainstream Discourses often incorporate attitudes and values hostile to, and even in part define themselves in opposition to, these minority students and their home- and community-based Discourses.

This difficulty of accommodation can certainly give rise to large problems in gaining the social goods that the society ties to mastery of mainstream Discourses, but it can also lead to reflective insight and metaknowledge (even in the absence of equitable or successful classroom teaching). Metaknowledge is power, because it leads to the ability to manipulate, to analyze, to resist while advancing. Such metaknowledge can make "maladapted" students smarter than "adapted" ones.

Today, attention to "process," "content," "meaning" as against the superficialities of "form" and "mechanical correctness" is a hallmark of "liberal," "humanist" approaches to writing instruction, and education generally. Nancy Mack (1989, 162), for instance, says: "Good listeners pay attention to the meaning of an utterance and not its correctness—unless, of course, there is some ideological benefit to be gained by stressing the surface features of the language." And as far as acquisition goes, there is some sense to this.

Unfortunately, however, many middle-class, mainstream, status-giving Discourses often *do* stress surface features of language. Why? Precisely because such surface features are the best test as to whether one was apprenticed in the "right" place, at the "right" time, with the "right" people. Such surface features are exactly the parts of Discourses most impervious to overt instruction and are only fully mastered (acquired) when everything else in the Discourse is mastered. Since these Discourses are used as "gates" to ensure that the "right" people get to the "right" places in our society, such surface features are ideal. A native English speaker who writes in a petition or office memo: "If you cancel the show, all the performers would have did all that hard work for nothing" has signaled that he or she isn't the "right sort of person" (was not fully acculturated to the Discourse that supports this identity), and that signal stays meaningful long after the content of the memo is forgotten or even when the content was of no interest in the first place.

Now, one can certainly encourage students to simply "resist" such "superficial features of language." And, indeed, they will get to do so from the bottom of society, where their lack of mastery of such superficialities was meant to place them anyway. But, of course, the problem is that such "superficialities" cannot be taught in a regular classroom in any case; they can't be "picked up" later, outside the full context of an early apprenticeship (at home and at school) in "middle class-like," school-based ways of doing and being. That is precisely why they work so well as "gates."

This is also precisely the tragedy of E. D. Hirsch, Jr.'s (1987), much-talked about book *Cultural Literacy*—he is right that without having mastered an extensive list of trivialities people can be (and often are) excluded from "goods" controlled by dominant groups in the society; he is wrong that this can be taught (in a classroom of all places!) apart from the socially situated practices that these groups have incorporated into their homes and daily lives. There is a real contradiction here, and we ignore it at the peril of our students.

But there is a partial way out of this dilemma (there is no total way out without serious change of the social structure). We have seen that raising such concerns to *overt considerations* can lead not to acquisition certainly (although that must be going on too) but to learning, metaknowledge. Thus, the "liberal" classroom that avoids overt talk of form and superficialities, of how things work, as well as of their sociocultural-political basis, are no help. Such talk can be powerful so long as one never thinks that in talking about grammar, form, or superficialities, one is getting people to actually acquire Discourses (or languages, for that matter). And, of course, such talk is always political talk, but then the absence of such talk is itself a political act (choice, however tacit).[2]

Further, even when true acquisition is not possible, and it is not in many cases where students come into the game late and with little opportunity for real apprenticeships within dominant Discourses outside what they can get in the classroom, what I will call "*mushfake* Discourse" is possible. "Mushfake" is a term from prison culture (see Mack, 1989, 161–62, from whom I got the term) meaning to make do with something less when the real thing is not available. So when prison inmates make hats from underwear to protect their hair from lice, the hats are mushfake.

Elaborate craft items made from used wooden matchsticks are another example of mushfake.

By "mushfake Discourse," I mean partial acquisition coupled with metaknowledge and strategies to "make do." Such strategies might include always having a memo edited to ensure no plural, possessive, or agreement errors (such as "he ask" in the present tense), as well as active use of black-culture skills at "psyching out" interviewers or "rising to the metalevel" in an interview so that the interviewer is thrown off stride by having the rules of the game implicitly referred to in the act of carrying them out. We cannot pretend mushfake Discourse will put an end to the effects of racism or classism, nor that it will open all doors. We can hope it will open some doors, while helping to change the society in the process. It is, at least, something to do while "waiting for the revolution."

So I propose that we ought to produce "muskfaking," resisting students, full of metaknowledge. But isn't that to politicize teaching? A Discourse is an integration of saying, doing, and *valuing*, and all socially based valuing is political. All successful teaching, that is, teaching that inculcates Discourse and not just content, is political. That is simply a truism.

DISCOURSES AND EDUCATION

A central concern in education today is in the question of why children from some minority groups fail in school at a disproportionate rate as compared to children from "mainstream," middle-class white culture. This topic, in fact, exemplifies in important ways the themes about Discourses that I have been developing in this chapter. However, let me begin to get at the issues here by initially discussing the unlikely topic of *phonics*.

Educators have been debating for decades whether schools ought to teach phonics or not, and this debate is a good example of how educational debates typically become polarized around opposite ends of a political spectrum (Adams, 1990; Chall, 1967). Proponents of phonics are perceived as "back-to-basics," reactionary conservatives; antiphonics proponents are perceived as progressive, permissive liberals coddling children. The fact of the matter is that we know a good many successful ways to teach any child to read. We even perfectly well know the answer to the phonics question, and it doesn't remotely fall into these stereotypes of liberal and conservative camps. Next to no interesting issue in literacy education does.

Innumerable studies have been done on the phonics question and innumerably more on other curricular questions. The most robust result of this immense research, as far as I can see, is the following (Adams, 1990; Chall, Jacobs, & Baldwin, 1990; Tharp & Gallimore, 1988). The success of a curriculum has less to do with its nature than with whether the people teaching it believe in it, advocate it, and see themselves as innovating it. Such people are reflective and involved when they teach; they lift difficulty ceilings and involve parents in education. They do so regardless of the particular philosophy or methods of their usually newly adopted program. Related to this fact is the additional fact that student engagement in literacy depends, more than anything else, on the momentum, support, and expectations created by the teacher.

Years ago I used work on the linguistics of American Sign Language and, connected with this interest, occasionally taught students who were going to become teachers of the deaf. As a linguist I realized that many methods of teaching deaf children English—for example, "cued speech," lip reading, various oral methods, invented sign systems, and other curricula that avoid American Sign Language are, *from a linguistic point of view*, quite unintelligent. I also knew that a robust result in the deaf education literature was that nearly *any* method, no matter how unintelligent it is, works *if* the teachers believe in it and the parents support it at home (Quigley & Paul, 1984). Let's be clear what all this means: it means that people who, from a scientific point of view, don't know what their doing, very often do just fine, *if* they strongly believe in what they're doing. The very best methods, without this strength of belief, fail miserably.

This result rather surprised me until I reflected on the fact that the *very best* teachers of school-based literacy the world has ever seen have never been trained and, from the point of view of educational science, have no idea what they are doing. And who are these master teachers? They are contemporary mainstream, middle- and upper-middle-class, "super baby"–producing parents. Under the great strain of the 1940s baby boom and the increased demand for spaces in the middle class and for ego-satisfying jobs, middle-class parents from the 1970s on have realized that they must actively *advantage* their children for school success by early home-based literacy practices (Toffler, 1990). What these parents have done and are doing works perfectly well, and we very well know *what* they are doing. We will look, a little later, at what it is they do.

So we must allow that enthusiasm and belief, advocacy and parental support, very often count for more than methods and research, regardless of what we say in our grant proposals. However, if we grant that we have enthusiasm (which, unfortunately, we very often don't), what is the answer to the heated phonics debate? Are the liberals or the conservatives right? They are both right, and they are both wrong.

The answer to the phonics question tells us something very important about child development, something we know from other sources as well. The answer to the question—now (and for some time, actually) supported by immense research is fourfold. I base my answer on my interpretation of Chall's work (Chall, 1967; Chall, Jacobs, & Baldwin, 1990) and Adams's (1990) masterful survey of the whole debate (see also Strickland & Cullinan's afterword to Adams's book, pp. 426–34, for a position similar to mine).

First, no one learns how to read, or knows how to read, who doesn't come to know, early and well, phonics in the sense of the relationship between the spoken code of the language and the written code. Second, leaving children to simply induce phonics by simple exposure to books, with no more overt scaffolding, is a waste of time, as much a waste of time as letting someone discover for themselves how to get to your house when you could give them a map—they may get there (and they may not), but it wasn't worth the effort.

Third, drilling students, especially minority students, on phonics rules, having them fill in missing letters on paper and pencil tests, and restricting them to basal readers and restricted literacy environments until they have mastered their "letters" is equally pointless and overtly harmful to boot. Fourth, no one learns to read, or knows how to read, who doesn't come to know, early and well, what one can *do* with print and what good it will do them to do it.

To see these principles in action, let's turn to a group of "teachers," many of whom manifestly succeed, namely, middle-class parents who incorporate "school-based" early literacy practices into their homes (Bruner, 1977, 1988; Cazden, 1988; Graff, 1987; Heath, 1983; Rogoff, 1990; Rose, 1989; Snow, 1983). Study of these parents has been the basis of an "industry" of work on "emergent literacy" (for some examples, see Bissex, 1980; Clay, 1976; Schickendanz, 1986; Taylor, 1983; Teale, 1986; Teale & Sulzby, 1986; for an excellent study devoted to lower socioeconomic black children, see Taylor & Dorsey-Gaines, 1987).

Most of these parents couldn't remember more than two phonics rules even if you paid them; and few of them would care to teach their children one in any case. But none of them fails to make a *big deal* out of *the sound and the form* of the language, out of letters, and out of decoding print into sounds. And none of them remotely thinks that sounds and letters are the beginning or the end of literacy. They discovered, as far as I am concerned, the answer to the phonics question without carrying out any research whatsoever.

There is a paradox in the answer to the phonics question. The paradox is related to the old saying that "you have to have money to make money." Paradoxically, children need phonics practice (practice in letter-word-sound-syllable correspondences) to become literate, but *it benefits them only when they are already, in a sense, literate.* Furthermore, this practice can take a great many forms, many of which look like play, or like engaging in "real"-world activities, and none of which need be memorizing rules.

To see what I mean, consider the following: Ask a preschool child to break off the first phoneme of a word or syllable, say, the /p/ in "pink," and then pronounce what's left, for example, /ink/. Success on tasks like this one correlates very strongly with concurrent and future reading acquisition. Such tasks imply that the child not only knows how to effortlessly speak and understand the language, as all children do, but that the child is, in addition, aware at a *metalevel* of the *code* of the spoken language; namely, the child is aware that words are made up of individual sounds (which we call phonemes) and characteristic clusters of these sounds (which we call syllables). The child has structural *metaknowledge* that directly relates to the fact that our writing system is alphabetic, that is, based on letters corresponding to sounds and on clusters of letters that constitute common spelling patterns.

Some people have taken this to mean that the knowledge such tasks implicates is the all-important preliminary foundations for being able to read and, thus, that we should drill students on such tasks when they get to school. However, it turns out that children who succeed at these tasks succeed because they have already had extensive exposure to *print* in their home-based early literacy practices. They are already, in an important sense, to be explicated in the next section below, *literate*.

There is a very real and very important *circle* here: there is no getting literate without gaining metaknowledge of the spoken and written code, and there is no getting this knowledge without being literate. Drilling children on phonics who aren't already literate won't work; attempting to get them literate without an explicit focus on the code is equally misguided. The key to this paradox is that being literate is not primarily a matter of being able to read and write in the sense of encoding and decoding print. Being literate is *not* primarily a mental ability, but rather a social one. Once we see this—a truth foreign to our Western individualism and focus on "intelligence" and private capacities—the paradox disappears, and the trick behind the magic of "super babies" becomes clear. Perhaps, then, we can buy some of this magic for all children.

Mainstream parents very often spend a huge amount of time *practicing (school-based) literacy* with their children, and what this means is that they *mentor* or *apprentice* their children into certain Discourses that schools and the wider mainstream culture reward. They engage their children in conversations and keep them on a single topic even when the children can hardly talk at all (Snow, 1983, 1986). They play alphabet games, recite nursery rhymes, read books aloud with great affect. They ask their children "What's that?" and "What's that say?" of pictures in a book they've both seen a hundred times (Heath, 1983). They encourage children to pretend they can read when they can't; they let them manipulate magnetic letters on a refrigerator; and they get them to watch "Sesame Street" for hours on end. They send them to preschool and constantly relate what the children have seen or heard in books to the children's daily experience of the world.

Most important of all, they make clear to their children that *people like us* use language, think, value, and talk *in these ways, with these objects at these times and in these places.* They introduce their children to Discourses that have, for social, historical, political, and social reasons come to overlap their homes and our schools. These Discourses are not "natural" and "normal"—lots of other groups neither do them nor find them very senseful (Gee, 1990c; Graff, 1987; Heath, 1983; Rose, 1989; Scollon & Scollon, 1981; Smitherman, 1977; Street, 1984). Long before the child can decode print, she has become a member of one or more school-based literacy Discourses—ways of thinking, acting, valuing with words and objects—that undergird school-based and mainstream literacy practices.

It is one of the main results of current research on cognition that human beings *know only what they have practiced over and over again*, and when they cease to practice it, it turns out, they cease to be any good at it, though they continue to be quite good at talking about it *as if* they were still good at it doing it—a result that warms a linguist's heart (Scribner & Cole, 1981). And how much does a mainstream child practice these school-based literacy activities at home and in preschool prior to going to first grade? Adams (1990) estimates a good deal over 3,000 hours prior to first grade. In contrast, the child's first grade teacher will spend about 360 hours, with a group of 20 or more children, on such literacy activities. On the other hand, based on a recent study of a group of lower socioeconomic families (Teale, 1986), Adams estimates that these families spent 225 hours per child on early school-based sorts of literacy activities (25 hours of storybook experience and perhaps 200 hours of general guidance about the form and nature of print).

It is crucial to stress that these social practices are *not* a magic set of "methodologies." What is happening is that the child is being *socialized* into certain ways of being in the world, ways intimately connected to the sociocultural identity of the child's group, as well as to their power and status in the world. These children are not learning and their parents are not teaching *skills*, though the children are most certainly picking up skills as a concomitant to the apprenticeship process. When a parent asks a young child "What's that?" of a picture in a picture book, the parent is not, in fact, trying to teach the child (the skills of) how to answer "what questions." Rather, this is merely a small part of what the parent does with the child in order to introduce the child into a characteristic (socially and culturally specific) *way of doing things*, into a particular *form of life*, in this case, how people "like us" approach books (talk about, read, value, use, and integrate them with other activities).

If you want to see how important these practices are, consider for a moment the Bristol Language Project in Great Britain, a longitudinal study of the language development of a representative sample of children born in the Bristol area in the years 1969–70 and 1971–72 (Wells, 1981, 1985, 1986). The school success of these children at age 10 was found to relate strongly to the children's preparedness for literacy upon entry to school as judged by a Test of Knowledge of Literacy given at age five. The results of this test, in turn, related directly to early literacy practices in the home, the sort we have just been discussing, practices taking place long before the age of five. Finally, both these practices and the results of the Test of Knowledge of Literacy related most directly to the children's social class (the lower their class, the worse they did).

If the children's early home-based preparedness for literacy is still strongly predicting their success in school at age ten, then school itself is not having much of an impact, save "to make the rich richer and the poor poorer." Current research coming out of the project continues to show the same picture even in regard to foreign-language instruction (Skehan, 1989, 31–34): the success of these children at age 14 in foreign-language classes correlates quite highly with their family backgrounds, for example, social class and parental education.

SOME EXAMPLES

All real learning is a form of apprenticeship, and apprenticeships are always apprenticeships into Discourses. I want to exemplify the points I have been raising in this chapter by looking at three concrete examples of Discourses in action in educationally relevant ways. Then I want to close with an example of successful teaching.

The first example is just the one we discussed in Chapter 1—the five-year-old's birthday story. This story clearly shows what I mean about a child's being literate prior to knowing how to read and write (in the sense of being able to decode and encode print). I reprint the story from Chapter 1 below:

How the Friends Got Unfriend

Stanza One (Introduction)

1. This is a story
2. About some kids who were once friends
3. But got into a big fight
4. And were not

Stanza Two (Frame: Signaling of Genre)

5. You can read along in your storybook
6. I'm gonna read aloud

[story-reading prosody from now on]

Stanza Three (Title)

7. "How the Friends Got Unfriend"

Stanza Four (Setting: Introduction of Characters)

8. Once upon a time there was three boys 'n three girls
9. They were named Betty Lou, Pallis, and Parshin, were the girls
10. And Michael, Jason, and Aaron were the boys
11. They were friends

Stanza Five (Problem: Sex Differences)

12. The boys would play Transformers
13. And the girls would play Cabbage Patches

Stanza Six (Crisis: Fight)

14. But then one day they got into a fight on who would be which team
15. It was a very bad fight
16. They were punching
17. And they were pulling
18. And they were banging

Stanza Seven (Resolution 1: Storm)

19. Then all of a sudden the sky turned dark
20. The rain began to fall
21. There was lightning going on
22. And they were not friends

Stanza Eight (Resolution 2: Mothers Punish)

23. Then um the mothers came shooting out 'n saying
24. "What are you punching for?
25. You are going to be punished for a whole year"

Stanza Nine (Frame)

26. The end
27. Wasn't it fun reading together?
28. Let's do it again
29. Real soon!

Let's consider how this text relates to our theory of Discourse. The child had started by telling a story about her birthday, to various relatives, over a couple of days, presumably in her home-based, primary Discourse. Then, on a given day, in the course of repeated book-reading episodes, she reshapes this story into another genre. She incorporates aspects of the book-reading episode into her story. Note, for example, the introduction in stanza 1, the frame in stanza 2, the title in stanza 3, and then the start of the story proper in stanza 4. She closes the frame in stanza 9. Note as well the "literary" syntax of the story (for example, stanza 4). This overall structure and style shapes the text into "storybook reading," though, in fact, there is no book, and the child can't read (proponents of traditional accounts of literacy are going to have deep conceptual problems here, because they trouble themselves too much over things like books and decoding and not enough over social practices).

Supported by her mother and older sister, This five-year-old is mastering the Discourse of "storybook reading." But this Discourse is itself an aspect of apprenticeship in another, more mature Discourse, namely, "literature" (as well as, in other respects, "essayist Discourse," but that is *another* story).[3]

This child, when she goes to school to begin her more public apprenticeship into the Discourse of literature, will look like a quick study indeed. It will appear that her success was inevitable, given her native intelligence and verbal abilities. Her success was inevitable, indeed, but because of her earlier apprenticeship.

Note too how her mastery of this "storybook reading" Discourse leads to the incorporation of a set of values and attitudes (about gender and the naturalness of middle-class ways of behaving) that are shared by many other dominant Discourses in our society. This will facilitate the acquisition of other dominant Discourses, some that may, at first, appear quite disparate from "literature" or "storybook reading."

This little girl, at five, unable to read in the sense of being able to decode print, is already in a very real sense "literate"—she has mastered the form of several Discourses relevant to school success. She already, in fact, knows a good deal about sounds and letters, from other home practices, and she can benefit perfectly well from an overt focus on sounds, letters, syllables, spelling patterns, and words. Such a focus is a flashlight on a field that is already well in place, illuminating a narrow range of that field for further practice.

My next example is a "sharing time" story (Cazden, 1988; Michaels, 1981) told at school by a seven-year-old black girl from a lower socioeconomic background. This girl is now in her early teens, and she has not been particularly successful at school-based literacy. Below I give the black child's sharing time story, which I call "Cakes." Although "sharing time" stories are normally told while the teacher is in the classroom, in this case the teacher had been called out, and the child simply told the story to her peers.

This child's "sharing time" stories were not viewed as successful by her teachers, who thought she "rambled," "exaggerated," "contradicted herself," moved from topic to topic just to extend her turn, and was sometimes "confused." We know from research by Sarah Michaels and others (Michaels, 1981; Michaels & Collins, 1984; Cazden, 1988), that during "sharing time" teachers are listening for stories that are organized quite differently than the stories black children often tell. Thus, in a sense, teachers fail to "hear" the stories black children are actually telling (and hear, instead, "disorganized" versions of the stories they are listening for).

The stories that many middle-class children tell at sharing time, and which teachers are listening for, are organized in a linear, chronological, reportive fashion typical of a number of these children's home-based language practices. Such stories are not "literary" like the five-year-old's story above, nor are they like the stories many black children tell; rather, they are like little "news reports." Black children's stories also link to various home-based practices, but different ones, practices the school knows (and often cares) little about. In fact, the stories Black children tell are embedded in a very rich and historically very old context of specific verbal practices in black culture.

Cakes

Stanza 1

1. Today
2. it's Friday the thirteenth
3. an' it's bad luck day
4. an' my grandmother's birthday is on bad luck day

PART 1: MAKING CAKES

Stanza 2

5. an' my mother's bakin a cake
6. an' I went up my grandmother's house while my mother's bakin' a cake
7. an' my mother was bakin' a cheesecake
8. my grandmother was bakin a whipped cream cupcakes

Stanza 3

9. an' we bof went over my mother's house
10. an' then my grandmother had made a chocolate cake
11. an' then we went over my aunt's house
12. an' she had make a cake

Stanza 4

13. an' everybody had made a cake for nana
14. so we came out with six cakes

PART 2: GRANDMOTHER EATS CAKES

Stanza 5

15. last night
16. my grandmother snuck out
17. an' she ate all the cake
18. an' we hadda make more

Stanza 6

(she knew we was makin' cakes)

19. an' we was sleepin'
20. an' she went in the room
21. an' gobbled em up
22. an' we hadda bake a whole bunch more

Stanza 7

23. she said mmmm

24. she had all chocolate on her face, cream, strawberries
25. she said mmmm
26. that was good

Stanza 8

27. an' then an' then all came out
28. an' my grandmother had ate all of it
29. she said "what's this cheesecake doin' here"—she didn't like cheese-
    cakes
30. an' she told everybody that she didn't like cheesecakes

Stanza 9

31. an' we kept makin' cakes
32. an' she kept eatin' 'em
33. an' we finally got tired of makin' cakes
34. an' so we all ate 'em

PART 3: GRANDMOTHER GOES OUTSIDE THE HOME

(Nonnarrative Section, Frames 35–41)

Stanza 10

35. an' now
36. today's my grandmother's birthday
37. an' a lot o'people's makin' a cake again
38. but my grandmother is goin t'get her own cake at her bakery
39. an' she's gonna come out with a cake
40. that we didn't make
41. cause she likes chocolate cream

Stanza 11

42. an' I went t'the bakery with her
43. an' my grandmother ate cupcakes
44. an' an' she finally got sick on today
45. an' she was growling like a dog cause she ate so many cakes

Stanza 12

46. an' I finally told her that it was
47. it was Friday the thirteenth bad luck day. (Gee 1990c: 119–20)

Laid out in terms of its lines and stanzas, the overall organization of
the text is readily apparent. The text is in three parts: Part 1 about baking
cakes, Part 2 about the grandmother eating up the cakes, and Part 3 about
the grandmother getting her own cakes at the bakery. Just before the close
of the story, in stanza 10, the child engages in some nonnarrative,
expository material. This is typical of the child's storytelling: she often
places such material right before her final narrative stanza. Such material

has what the sociolinguist William Labov (1972b) has called an "evaluative" role; that is, it signals what in the storyteller's view makes the story "tellable," "significant," or "interesting."

The style of the language of the text is also fairly obvious, and recognizably part of a black cultural tradition (Smitherman, 1977). The child uses language in a "poetic," rather than a "prosaic" way; she tries to "involve" the audience, rather than just to "inform" them (Nichols, 1989). She uses considerable syntactic parallelism, repetition, and sound devices to set up rhythmic and poetic patterning within and across her stanzas. For example, stanzas 2 and 3 have the sort of structuring I have diagrammed below:

Stanza 2

5.		my mother's	bakin' a cake
6.	my grandmother's	my mother's	bakin' a cake
7.		my mother	bakin' an X cake
8.	my grandmother was		bakin' an X cake

Stanza 3

9.	we		went over my X's house
10.		Y had made a cake	
11.	we		went over my Z's house
12.		Z had made a cake	

Stanza 6 repeats line by line, with different language, the content of stanza 5; stanza 8 is just a "different take" on the same episode enacted by stanza 7. Stanza 4 is a two-line summary of all of Part 1, while stanza 9 is a four-line summary of all of Part 2. We can see clearly in stanza 2 that the child is working with structural formats. In this stanza she is working with the pattern: " . . . bakin' a cake / . . . bakin' a cake / . . . bakin' a Type of cake / . . . bakin' a Type of cake." But the last line involves a plural (cupcakes) and thus can't take the indefinite singular article "a." The girl, driven by the pattern, uses "a" anyway, a "speech error" that gives us some insight into the schemalike patterns that are helping to drive production and that are freeing her to invest cognitive energy in creating meaning and building larger patterns throughout the text as a whole.

Clearly, the narrator here is not primarily interested in making rapid and linear progress to "the point." Rather, she is interested in creating a pattern out of language, within and across her stanzas, much like a painting or a poem, a pattern that will generate meaning through the sets of relationships and contrasts it sets up, like the multiple relationships and contrasts, points of contact and stress, in a painting or a poem.

And what might that meaning be? Of course, there are always multiple plausible interpretations of a text (and many nonplausible ones as well). But if we follow the clues or guides the child has placed in the organization of her text and are sensitive to the child's culture, we can offer a "reading" that accepts the invitations of her text.

The nonnarrative "evaluative" section in stanza 10 suggests that there is something significant in the fact that the grandmother is going to get a cake at the bakery and thus "come out with a cake that we [the family] didn't make." And, indeed, the story as a whole places a great deal of emphasis on the production of cakes within the family, a production that doesn't cease even when the grandmother keeps eating them. The grandmother, the matriarch and repository of the culture's norms, is behaving like a child, sneaking out and eating the cakes and rudely announcing that she doesn't like "cheesecake" even though the cake has been made by her relatives for her birthday. It must intrigue the child narrator that the grandmother can behave this way and, far from getting in trouble, the family simply makes more cakes. Surely the story carries some messages about family loyalty and respect for age.

But it also, I would argue, raises a problem: the matriarch, the guardian of culturally normative behavior, is behaving in such a way as to violate the home and culture's canons of polite behavior. What might the sanctions be for such a violation? And what is the deeper meaning of the grandmother's violation? Like all real stories, this one raises real problems, problems that the story attempts to resolve (in large part through its structure) in a satisfying manner.

We can get to this deeper level of the text if we consider the constant use of and play on the word "cake" in the story. The story, in fact, contains a humorous paradox about cakes: the grandmother eats innumerable (normal-sized) cakes at home, made by her relatives, and never gets sick. Then she goes outside the home, buys little cakes ("cupcakes") at the bakery, and not only does she get sick, she "growls like a dog," that is, loses her human status and turns into an animal. Why?

What I would argue is this: the grandmother is learning, and the child narrator is enacting, a lesson about *signs* or symbols. A birthday cake is a material object, but it is also an immaterial sign or symbol of kinship, *when made within the family*—a celebration of birth and family membership. The cake at the bakery looks the same, but it is a duplicitous symbol—it is not actually a sign of kinship; rather it is a commodity that non-kin have made to sell, not to celebrate the birth of someone they care about. To mistake the baker's cake as a true symbol of birth and kin is to think, mistakenly, that signs have meaning outside the contexts that give them meaning. In the context of the family, the cake means kinship and celebration; in the context of the bakery and market society, it signals exchange and commodities.

The grandmother, in her greed, overvalues the material base of the sign (its cakehood) and misses its meaning, undervaluing the network of kin that gives meaning to the cakes. This is particularly dangerous when we consider that the grandmother is a senior representative of the family and culture. Her penalty is to momentarily lose her human status, that is, the status of a giver and taker of symbolic meaning—she becomes an animal, merely an eater. The grandmother's behavior and its consequences are the product of fate—it's Friday the thirteenth, bad luck day—rooted in the "nature" of things, not merely a matter of social conventions (a view shared by all cultures, as far as I can see, including our schools, which take their literacy practices to be "ahistorical," "natural," and "inevitable," practices people can fail at only if they are "deprived").

And now, of course, I must face the same question that could have been raised in regard to the five-year-old's story: could this seven-year-old really have meant this? Could she really have this sophisticated a theory of signs? I would argue that these questions seem so compelling to us because we have a much less good theory of signs than this child has. We think meaning is a matter of privatized intentions locked in people's heads and indicative of their individual "intelligence" or "skill." But once we deny this view of meaning, the questions lose most of their force; in fact, they become somewhat odd.

This little girl has inherited, by her apprenticeship in the Discourses of her community, ways of making sense of experience that, in fact, have a long and rich history going back thousands of years. This enculturation/apprenticeship has given her certain *forms of language*, ranging from devices at the word and clause level, through the stanza level, to the story level as a whole, forms of language that are intimately connected to *forms of life*.

These forms of language are not merely structural. Rather, they encapsulate, carry through time and space, *meaning*, meanings shared by and lived out in a variety of ways by the social group. The girl speaks the language, engages in the Discourse, and gets the meanings "free": she is a "carrier" of the Discourse. It is a good performance, indeed, and it should be: the little girl is apprenticed to a group that has been working on it for hundreds of years. It's just a shame that it doesn't "sell" in our schools, which unfortunately accept a view of signs much closer to the grandmother's momentary lapse.

SUCCESSFUL TEACHING/RESEARCH

My third example moves us to the classroom and raises very important issues about testing and evaluation. It is also a good example of the close relationship that exists between good ethnography of education and good teaching. They are often very similar activities.

The example comes from a third-fourth, multi-ethnic classroom in Cambridge, Massachusetts, and was discussed in a recent paper by my colleague Sarah Michaels (1990). The class is doing a science activity using a little beam balanced on a small upright pole; the beam has small metal weights of various values placed on it at different points. The students have been asked to predict, by a class vote, whether, with the weights where they are, the balance will tip to the right, to the left, or stay balanced. The students vote for their choice, then debate or discuss their predication with each other as a group. After the discussion, they revote, in case they have changed their minds on the basis of someone else's explanation. Finally, the teacher demonstrates the actual experiment.

During the discussion, a student named Erik is asked why he thinks the beam will balance. Since there are two weights on the right, each with a value of 5, and on the left are three weights with a value of 3 each and one weight with the value of 1, Eric says, "Okay, well there's 10 on the right, cause 2 times 5 is 10, and (on the left) three times 3 is 9, and then you just do 1 times 1, is 1, and 1 and 9 is 10, so it will balance."

Then Elizabeth, a Haitian girl and native speaker of Haitian Creole, asks for a turn. Erik, the previous speaker, calls on her. The following interaction between Elizabeth and the teacher now ensues:

ELIZABETH: I agree with you and Neirika and Semhar, because I, I was thinking it will tip to the [right], it will, um, be balance[d].

TEACHER: And what was making you think that?

ELIZABETH: Because, I was only sitting down and I say, um, remember, um, . . . I think it will be balanced . . . I think, and I think it will be balanced because I was thinking and I say it will tip to the [right], I say, I think, and I think it will be balanced.

TEACHER: So do you remember what made you think that? Were you just persuaded by, were you persuaded by what other children were able to say?

ELIZABETH: [*nods head no*] Un uh.

TEACHER: Or were you thinking that, can you give us some words for this thinking?

ELIZABETH: I think um, well, I was sitting down like this, and I was thinking, in my head, I think it will tip to the right, but after I been thinking a lot, I think it will balance.

At this point the teacher gives up and asks Elizabeth to pick someone else to speak. Later, a classroom ethnographer who had been studying this lesson asks Elizabeth some more questions, allowing her to first answer in Haitian and then to "translate" her answer into English. The following dialogue ensued:

ETHNOGRAPHER: Can you tell me why you thought it would balance or why you now think it would balance?

ELIZABETH: [*After her Haitian answer, she says "I say" and continues*] because I was thinking in my brain, and my brain think it will be balance, and it's . . . I say that.

ETHNOGRAPHER: Okay, now I'm gonna ask you another question. Why? Say more about why.

ELIZABETH: [*looks puzzled*) Say more about why?

ETHNOGRAPHER: Why do you think it will be balanced? What did your brain think to get you to think it would be balanced?

ELIZABETH: I don't know because I didn't ask my brain.

ETHNOGRAPHER: Ask your brain about the weights and where they are and why you think it would be balanced or why you think it did balance.

ELIZABETH: [*After a couple of more turns with the ethnographer, and with her actually putting the weights on the right places, she says*] Because you know after I think it would be balanced, I tried it, . . . and it's right, ta da!

ETHNOGRAPHER: Okay, I'm gonna still keep pushing you on this, this is very helpful, but why does it have to balance? Why doesn't it tip to the right or to the left?

ELIZABETH: [*saying this as if the ethnographer is really dumb*]: Because I make um multiplication in my head [*and then without a moment's hesitation, she walks the ethnographer right through the appropriate multiplication in both Creole and English*].

The ethnographer then asks Elizabeth why she didn't tell her all the "multiplication stuff" in the first place when she had asked Elizabeth why it would balance. Elizabeth says, quietly, "I didn't understand your question." The problem that Elizabeth has here is not in her ability to reason or in her control of the requisite multiplication skills. She knows her multiplication facts cold and knows how to apply them to reason through problems like this one.

What Elizabeth fails to know and control is the Discourse of school science. She interpreted the teacher's *why* questions and the ethnographer's initial *why* questions as asking about the status of her knowledge as final product—was it a guess, was she simply accepting what her classmates said, or had she figured the answer out by herself?— not as asking about the steps by which she had computed the answer. Elizabeth repeatedly answers the question *she* hears and not the one the teacher hears herself as asking. However, in the Discourse of school science, in order to count as having figured something out by yourself, you have to "rerun" your reasoning in front of the teacher, making your reasoning public and explicit.

Elizabeth doesn't need training in multiplication; she needs someone to actively apprentice her in the Discourse of school science. As she builds up the ability to engage in this Discourse—in thought, word, and deed—practice with math and other technical matters will make sense and will take hold, just as phonics will take hold when sown in an already fertile field of membership in literacy-based Discourses, and not otherwise.

Elizabeth's case also shows up the failure of standard school testing and evaluation. She would have failed any typical school test of this lesson—but, in fact, she had the requisite knowledge. What the ethnographer did was *interactively scaffold* Elizabeth until this knowledge emerged. Elizabeth showed that together with the ethnographer she could come up with the right sort of language. Later she will be able to do this by herself. This is a good example of *developmental evaluation*: working interactively with children to see what they can do with support. In such a process the child learns and develops, and we learn what the child is "ready" for, what she will soon be able to do by herself if we give her the necessary support.

The ethnographer was scaffolding (supporting) Elizabeth, helping her to do with the ethnographer what she could not accomplish alone (engage in answering school science questions). But I have argued above that there is also a role for explicit teaching—telling people exactly what they need to know. However, such teaching must be directed to minds already prepared through having begun and been supported in apprenticeships within requisite Discourses. The ethnographer was engaged in just such a master-apprenticeship relationship with Elizabeth.

Thus, I want to close by giving you what I consider to be an excellent example of explicit teaching. The example demonstrates one crucial role that teachers must play if children are to master school-based Discourses. But to explicate this role, I must (alas) tell a personal anecdote. Humans can recognize natural beauty, that is, beauty in other people and in nature. And they can come to appreciate the beauty of the artificial creations that we call "art," things like painting or music. However, there is no reason to believe humans can learn to appreciate the beauty of painting, for instance, just by going to a class on the aesthetics of painting or on art history. Plenty of people have taken such classes and are now bored stiff in a museum confronted by a painting and not a test.

Indeed, I confess that I was such a person. Though I had had classes on aesthetics and art history, and though I had read books on painting, I was quite puzzled about why anyone would like Cézanne's paintings, for example. This bothered me because the art books said Cézanne was "the father of modern art" (Lorne, 1943). So I once spent months reading books on modern art and standing in front of the few Cézanne's in the National Museum of Art in Washington. I felt I got nowhere, though I kept looking at and studying these paintings and other examples of modern art.

Discouraged, I returned to Boston, feeling quite the philistine, and quite ready to concede defeat. It so happened that upon my return to Boston a friend of mine wanted to go to the Boston Museum of Fine Arts. While I was standing in front of the museum's (at the time) sole Cézanne and telling my companion my sad story, bemoaning the fact that the painting meant nothing to me, an elderly Irish museum guard came up to us and pointed to the painting and said: "Isn't that a great painting?"

Embarrassed, I timidly said, "sure." He then said, "You see how the way that table there is purple, which makes it jut out from its background and seem so solid so that . . .", and on he went telling me what the purple of the table did in the painting. As he spoke, I looked at the table and the painting as a whole, and all of a sudden it made sense. I finally saw it, how the painting worked, how Cézanne worked. Cézanne's paintings seemed at that moment, and have ever since, very wonderful indeed.

What the guard had done was most certainly an act of teaching. After much thought and practice on my own in a natural setting, that is, in front of paintings, the guard called my attention to, focused my attention on, a piece of the data that I was ready at that point to understand and to relate to everything else I had unconsciously been learning. A piece of the system of modern painting fell into place in my mind at that point, rendering me able to go on, on my own, to learn more about art in general by looking at paintings.

Perhaps I would have finally paid attention to that piece of data, or one like it, and the system would have jelled. Probably I would have given up and, when forced into a museum, would then have been one of those people who, standing in front of a masterpiece, say, "My five-year-old could have painted that."

When I asked the guard how he knew so well how to "introduce" me to the painting, he said that he had noticed in twenty-five years as a guard at the museum that art tours always stopped at that painting. He has listened to twenty-five years of lectures and comments on the painting. That is not, of course, what made him a great teacher. What made him a great teacher is that he knew when and where to strike to get me to see what I needed to see.

Teachers can, at the right moment, point to the right fact, focus the learner's attention on the right thing to look at, to pay attention to at that moment, out of the myriad of things he or she could pay attention to. Good teachers do this all the time, though they don't know they are doing it. Good textbooks do it all the time, though their authors don't think that's what they are doing. There aren't, however, lots of good teachers or good textbooks, and good textbooks are a menace in the hands of teachers who aren't good teachers.

In any case there is evidence that focusing learners on the right input at the right time, namely, when they are ready for it and when they have practiced in natural settings, is a form of teaching that can be successful. Phonics is, in fact, like the purple of Cézanne's table: It is necessary to see it, but it is meaningless and trivial unless you've spent time in a museum; if you have, then it is anything but trivial.

Schools must supply rich, interactive apprenticeships in Discourses to all children, and they must have teachers who know where and how to say "Look at *that*" (where "that" may very well be "when two vowels go walking, the first does the talking" or stripping a /p/ off of the word "pink") at the right time and place. But it does no good to tell people to look at what they cannot see. And we can see only what has already been opened up for our view by an apprenticeship within some Discourse that renders such things "visible" in the first place.

NOTES

1. In second-language research the distinction between acquisition and learning is most often associated with the work of Stephen Krashen (see 1985a, b). For critical discussion of Krashen's work, and a general discussion of theories of second-language development, see McLaughlin (1987). On why first languages are not "learned," but "acquired," see Chomsky (1986, 1988); and Pinker (1989). I should make it clear that I am using the terms "acquisition" and "learning" in a somewhat different way than Krashen and that I do not fully endorse his theory of second-language acquisition. I am not here talking about language acquisition, but something much broader, namely, the acquisition of Discourses.

2. I have in mind here many classroom approaches that go by such names as "process writing," "whole language approaches," "open classrooms," and many others. I am *not* condemning any of these approaches, nor arguing for "traditional" approaches or any "back-to-basics" movement. Further, it turns out that many different things actually go on in classrooms under the rubric of "process writing." But we should be aware that failing to focus on "forms," and stressing "meaning" and the student's own "voice," can privilege those students who already know the "rules" and the "forms," especially if grades are assigned partly on how well the writing ultimately matches traditional expectations, either in the "process writing" class itself or in later, more content-based classes it is "preparing" the students for. The "process writing" class exists in an overall system, and it can become complicit with that system in replicating the hierarchical status quo in yet another form, and one that is, perhaps, more effective in that the students who fail, fail without understanding the basis of the system that failed them. The grading and overall evaluation system is "mystified" by the focus on processes, voice, and meaning in the "process writing" class, a focus that often does not represent the rest of the overall educational system in which the "process writing" class is situated, and, indeed, one that is not always consistently practiced in the class itself. I do not believe in any particular methodology, nor in "methodological fixes." Rather, I believe many methodologies work when they are coupled with the sort of sociocultural and political awareness hinted at in the text (see Delpit, 1986, 1988; and Willinsky, 1990, for an interesting discussion in regard to these issues).

3. Wanda Giles, in regard to the five-year-old's story, remarks that the five-year-old "is, of course, a girl. Her compliance is notable." She comments that there are, in this book, no boys who are equally encouraged toward verbalizing and storybook reading—"the one a stereotypical female trait/habit, the second something that suggests the decorative arts." She notes, too, that the audience in the episode is itself all female. The point is well taken. Most of the studies on the early apprenticeships that middle-class families offer their children into school-based Discourses (well summarized in Rogoff, 1990) stress specific culturally based verbal skills and approaches to narratives and

stories but fail to get at important gender differences in these appenticeships. It is often said that early storybook reading (of a certain type) is quite important for later school success for both girls and boys (for example, Wells, 1986), but it would be useful to know how early storybook reading differs along gender lines (both of parent and child).

CONCLUSION: THE SOCIAL MIND

The major theme of this book has been that, in our everyday lives and in much traditional psychology, what we think of as "mental" is, in fact, "social." Meaning and memory, believing and knowing, are social practices that vary as they are embedded within different Discourses within a society. Each Discourse apprentices its members and "disciplines" them so that their mental networks of associations and their folk theories converge towards a "norm" reflected in the social practices of the Discourse. These "ideal" norms, which are rarely directly statable, but only discoverable by close ethnographic study, are what constitute meaning, memory, believing, knowing, and so forth, from the perspective of each Discourse. The mental networks in our heads, as well as our general cognitive processing abilities, are tools that we each use to get in and stay in the social "games" our Discourses constitute.

We have seen, in Chapter 5, that any Discourse is defined in terms of who *is* and who *is not* a member, and sometimes in terms of who are "higher" and "lower," more "central" and "less central" members. Discourses can even have "colonized" members. Furthermore, as we also saw in the last chapter, any Discourse is ultimately defined in *relationship* to and, often, in *opposition* to, other Discourses in the society.

If we define "politics" as *relationships and interactions among people where power and status are at stake*, then practices within and across Discourses are always and everywhere *political*. If we define "ideology" as *beliefs about the appropriate distribution of social goods, such as power, prestige, status, distinction, or wealth,* then Discourses are always and everywhere *ideological.* Each Discourse necessitates that members, at least while they are playing roles within the Discourse, act as if they hold particular beliefs and values about what counts as the "right sort" of person and the "right" way to be in the world, and thus too, what counts as the "wrong" sort and the "wrong" way. And "right" here means "worthy of respect and status," both social goods.

I want to close this book by exemplifying these claims about the political and ideological nature of Discourses through an analysis of a single text. This analysis will also bring together many of the points made in this book as a whole. It will also demonstrate that there is no way to study language, meaning, or the mind apart from the inherently ideological and political nature of Discourses.

This text was written by a ninth-grade Puerto Rican inner-city junior-high-school girl. The students at this girl's school (in the eastern United States) are drawn in roughly equal numbers from adjacent working and lower-socioeconomic Black, white, and Puerto Rican neighborhoods. The text is reprinted from Amy Shuman's 1986 study of the uses of oral and written texts by urban adolescents, *Storytelling Rights* (9–11). The girl, whom Shuman calls pseudonymously Wilma, offered this unsolicited account of her three years at the school toward the end of Shuman's research.

Wilma describes her first day of school in each grade and compares her lack of familiarity with the system in the seventh grade with her mastery of it by the ninth grade. I first reproduce the initial part of Wilma's text (devoted to seventh grade) as she wrote it, with no "corrections." Below that, I give a summary (with some direct quotes) of the parts of the text devoted to the eighth and ninth grades. Finally, I present the first part of Wilma's text again, this time in the form of "lines" and "stanzas."

In other work (Gee, 1986, 1989c, 1990b) I have argued that all speech and much writing falls into such lines and stanzas and that such structures are part of the human language processing mechanism. While all speakers use lines and stanzas, speakers from different sociocultural groups pattern language within stanzas in different ways. I am not here concerned with the psycholinguistic nature of lines and stanzas. For our purposes here, displaying Wilma's text in terms of its lines and stanzas simply makes it easier to appreciate and analyze.

Seventh Grade

When I first came to Paul Revere I was kind of scared but it was going to be my first year there but I was supposed too get used too going there. I started early in the Morning I was happy. Everybody talking about it sounded scarry, and nice. A couple of us caught the bus together. When we got there, since I was a seventh grader I was supposed to go to the audotorium—which I did. from there I appeared in the boy's gym. I didn't knew until they announced where we were at. From there I appeared somewhere else. That was my home room. Which they called advisory. I copy something from the board called a Roster. After that a Bell rang. We waited for another Bell and left. I met with my friends and cought the bus back home. They explained how to used the rosters. Which I learned very quickly.

The Classroom I was in like a regular elementary school which was only from one room to the other. I didn't understand that. Until our teacher explained that was called Mini School. Well we did a lot of things. Went on a lot of trips. And were treated fairly by both teachers.

I didn't hardly had any friends until I started meeting a lot of them. I had a friend by the name of Luisa and Alicia. Those were the only two friends I had at the beginning of the year. Almost at the middle I met one girl by the name of Barbara. We were starting to get real closed to each other and were starting to trust each other. As you know we still are very closed and trust each other.

Wilma
(Shuman 1986:9)

Summary of 8th and 9th grades

Eighth Grade

On the first day, Wilma and Barbara were placed in the same class. They cut the first day of classes and on the second day noticed that they didn't know very many people in their class. But then they met more and more people and it looked like it was going to be "a super year." Everybody was getting along and "[t]here were no argument between races or color." They cut school a great deal and "did not obey the teacher. Since that was our second year and we know the school by heart we didn't bother. We were really bad made almost all the teachers had a hard time with us." Wilma concludes: "I enjoy this year very much, had a nice time and enjoy every bit of it."

Ninth Grade

Barbara and Wilma thought they would be assigned to different classes but are overjoyed when they are not (Wilma writes: "I jump with such of joy that I thought that was going to be the end of us"). They are in a class with a strict teacher. Wilma likes it because the teacher reviews "what you had in the 7th and 8th grades." She concludes: "Like I say if you could hang until something thats very strict you do alright. But don't let her take over you at all. Stay quite when she talks to you in front of the class but when it by your self and her let everything out and you'll get everything your way."

"Seventh Grade" in Lines and Stanzas

PART I: SCHOOL

IA: GOING TO SCHOOL

Stanza 1

When I first came to Paul Revere
I was kind of scared
but it was going to be my first year there
but I was supposed too get used too going there.

Stanza 2

I started early in the Morning
I was happy.
Everybody talking about it sounded scarry, and nice.
A couple of us caught the bus together.

IB: MOVING FROM PLACE TO PLACE

Stanza 3

When we got there,
since I was a seventh grader
I was supposed to go to the audotorium
—which I did.

Stanza 4

From there I appeared in the boy's gym.
I didn't knew until they announced where we were at.
From there I appeared somewhere else.
That was my home room.
Which they called advisory.

IC: ENDING THE DAY AND GOING HOME

Stanza 5

I copy something from the board called a Roster.
After that a Bell rang.
We waited for another Bell and left.

Stanza 6

I met with my friends
and cought the bus back home.

They explained how to used the rosters.
Which I learned very quickly.

PART II: THE CLASS GENERALLY

Stanza 7

The Classroom I was in like a regular elementary school
which was only from one room to the other.
I didn't understand that.
Until our teacher explained that was called Mini School.

Stanza 8

Well we did a lot of things.
Went on a lot of trips.
And were treated fairly by both teachers.

PART III: FRIENDS

Stanza 9

I didn't hardly had any friends
until I started meeting a lot of them.
I had a friend by the name of Luisa and Alicia.
Those were the only two friends I had at the beginning of the year.

Stanza 10

Almost at the middle I met one girl by the name of Barbara.
We were starting to get real closed to each other
and were starting to trust each other.
As you know we still are very closed and trust each other.

Faced with any text, it is absolutely crucial to place it within its appropriate Discourse (Alverson & Rosenberg, 1990; Gee 1990a; Labov & Fanshel, 1977). Often texts like Wilma's are treated as if they were failed attempts at a school-based "essayist" Discourses. In "scientific" studies in educational research, texts like Wilma's are compared, as examples of "bad writing," with texts which exemplify "good writing." Such texts are "coded" for variables like spelling and other mechanics of writing, or markers of cohesion, and found to be "different" and "lacking" in regard to "good writing." But such comparisons are utterly meaningless, since Wilma is *not*, it turns out, writing for or within any school-based Discourse.

To compare Wilma's text to school-based, "essayist" writing would be like comparing someone playing baseball with someone playing football and claiming that one was doing something well that the other was failing at. To say that a baseball player is playing bad football or that a football player is playing baseball poorly would be absurd. They are simply engaged in different activities. But we do such things in regard to texts like Wilma's all the time.

The adolescents in Wilma's school use both speaking and writing to make sense of their experiences. Traditional approaches to literacy assume that speaking is used for face-to-face communication and writing for absent-author communication. But the adolescents in Wilma's school often use oral stories to convey messages to absent third parties through "he-said-she-said" rumors that will be repeated back to them, and they often use writing as part of face-to-face exchanges in which documents are collaboratively produced and read aloud or as solitary communication with oneself in dairies.

Shuman points out that "the adolescents transformed the conventional uses of writing and speaking for their own purposes. They had their own understanding of what could be written but not said, and vice versa" (1989: 3). But note the use of the word "conventional" here—what is being called "conventional" is *not* Wilma's group's uses of writing and reading; in fact, her group has a different convention. "Conventional" here means "some dominant group's uses of writing."

The fact is that Wilma and her peers have a community-based secondary Discourse, used in the community and at school, that employs speaking and writing (notes, diaries, letters) of various sorts to signal a particular social identity. This Discourse is used by adolescents from black, Puerto Rican, and lower socioeconomic white groups. It is used in the school yard, on the way to and from school, in the community when adolescent peers come together, and at school for "off-line" communication not under the school's control.

I call such Discourses "borderland Discourses" because they are situated in the borderland between the home and the school (Gee, 1990c). These adolescents live in different, largely segregated neighborhoods around their common school. They come together—blacks, Puerto Ricans, and lower socioeconomic whites—only at the intersections of their neighborhoods, on the way to and from school, in the school yard, and in school. As Wilma's text points out ("[t]here were no argument between races or color"), there is always the potential for tension among these different cultural groups.

Yet, between school and home, these adolescents are friends and peers. They are also tied together through their common knowledge that the decaying urban school they attend represents a statement about the value the wider society places on them and their communities. They mutually know also that the school represents an institution whose Discourses are dominated by values and interests often more in the service of the elites of the society than their own.

Or perhaps I should say that this sort of mutual knowledge is always open to them for discovery in the very material, economic, and social conditions in which they live. Furthermore, the school has been a site at which their identities and interests, and those of their communities, have often been denigrated, ignored, or misunderstood. This borderland Discourse has been developed by these adolescents themselves. It conflicts with school-based Discourses at various points and, indeed, partly defines itself by these conflicts and oppositions. Wilma's text must be read in terms of *this Discourse*.

But Wilma's text is not a "pure" instance of this secondary Discourse (in the real world of interaction in which Discourses are always jostling against each other, there are few "pure" instances). It was written for Shuman, who, though familiar with the girls and their social practices, was still a "mainstream" outsider (and further, an academic and thus connected to school-based Discourses).

Shuman points out that the text presents "one form of adolescent writing: in this case, a document intended for outside readers already familiar with the general situation but not with the details of personal experience" (1989: 9), and "Wilma's description of her school years contained the same kinds of observations girls made in their diaries, but as a separate document it was the only account of its kind I saw in my three years of research at the school. In its attention to the unwritten rules of the adolescent's conventions for written texts, it is perhaps typical" (p. 11).

That is, Wilma is using her community-based borderland secondary Discourse, but adapting it to an aspect of a mainstream school-based Discourse, namely, the "separate" document that is not in note, dairy, or letter form. She is undoubtedly influenced in this adaptation by other aspects of school-based essayist Discourse as well, though without very careful study we can't know exactly at which points (and, thus, can't say with any certainty what is a "mistake" in a Discourse she does not fully control and what is just a part of Wilma's practice within her borderland Discourse).

It is crucial to situate Wilma's text, then, within the interactional style, the values, and beliefs of her borderland Discourse. To a certain extent we can, in fact, use such texts to make hypotheses about what the values of this Discourse are and then check these hypotheses against richer ethnographic study. It is clear from Wilma's text that she defines her membership within her borderland Discourse in relationship to and partly in opposition to the school and its Discourses. Note in this respect that of the eighth grade Wilma says, "We were really bad made almost all the teachers had a hard time with us," but nonetheless, "I enjoy this year very much, had a nice time and enjoy every bit of it," and note also that in the ninth grade she says, "But don't let her [the teacher] take over you at all."

It is also clear that *trust* is a big concern for Wilma within her Discourse. She trusts her peers within the Discourse but is suspicious of the school and its intents. Note in the seventh grade she concludes that "[we] were treated fairly by both teachers"—hardly a remark that would need to be made if it were not the case that Wilma assumes some teachers will not treat her and her group fairly. On the other hand, Wilma's close and trusting relationship with Barbara is a major theme throughout all the years of the schooling she reports.

If we consider for a moment the fully reproduced part of Wilma's text above ("the seventh grade"), we can see yet other themes relevant to her Discourse. This story about the seventh grade is supposed to set the scene (by showing her initial incompetence) for her later discussion of the eighth and ninth grades, which stress her competence and control. Note how Wilma starts her story of the seventh grade, in her first paragraph, by going to school with her friends ("A couple of us caught the bus together"). Arriving at the school, she is separated from her friends and has to confront the school alone (she wanders from room to room not knowing where she is or what to do and confronts a "strange" practice of the school—the rosters). But eventually she is reunited with her friends for the return home, and they explain to her how to use the rosters (a technique she learns quickly).

Here we see Wilma confronting the new and foreign (and possibly hostile) Discourse of the school and classroom. She is initiated into this Discourse and helped initially not by the school, but by her friends (her own community), whose Discourse is in conflict with the school (and vice versa), but which is nonetheless used to initiate Wilma into school practices.

In her second paragraph, Wilma juxtaposes her friends' help with the teachers' help (they explain her classroom and treat her fairly). There is the hint here that Wilma can utilize the teachers' and the school's help only through the support given her by her own community. As if to stress this, Wilma returns at the end of her story, in her third paragraph, to friends, closing on her new friendship with Barbara (who figures prominently in the next two stories). School is seen, not as a place to just learn, but as a place to forge more friendships within the borderland

Discourse that supports her presence at school and mediates her relationship with the school. Notice that Wilma's paragraphing makes perfect sense in terms of her own thematics.

If we now look at the line and stanza structure of this part of the text, we can see yet more of its thematics. Wilma devotes two stanzas to "going to school," then two stanzas to "moving from place to place within the school," then two stanzas to the "roster," a practice of the school (stanza 5) that is explained to her by her peers on the way home, in the borderland (stanza 6). Then Wilma devotes two stanzas to her teachers instructing her, directly contrasting this instruction to the peer-based instruction in the preceding two stanzas. She ends on two stanzas devoted to her forming friendships (stanza 9 devoted to friendships generally, and stanza 10 devoted to Barbara, who will be a major figure in the following years).

For Wilma, then, the *initiation* into school is set in motion by her peers accompanying her to school and instructing her in regard to its strange practices, and the *culmination* of her first year is the formation of trusting friendships within her borderland Discourse. The middle is devoted to wandering from place to place and finally getting instruction from her teachers, specific teachers who treat Wilma's group "fairly." The beginning and end are rooted in her peers and her peer-based borderland Discourse. School, for Wilma, is not just or primarily about apprenticeship into school-based Discourses; it is about apprenticeship and membership into her borderland Discourse.

Notice how wonderfully Wilma captures in stanza 4 the sense of going from place to place without knowing where you are: "From there I appeared in the boy's gym. I didn't knew until they announced where we were at. From there I appeared somewhere else. That was my home room. Which they called advisory." She just "pops up" places—no one in the school is making this terrain accessible to her understanding. In Wilma's world of segregated neighborhoods, conflicting groups, and a school that does not represent the interests of her communities, knowing where you are (literally) and where you stand (figuratively) is important. School is a threat in part because it is "not her place" yet. Eventually, through her first year, she and her group colonize the school, rendering it a familiar place through the services of their borderland Discourse.

Notice that by the second year, she says "that was our second year and we know the school by heart." Knowing the school by heart means that they "cut school a great deal" and that they "didn't bother. We were really bad made almost all the teachers had a hard time with us." That is, it means that they devoted their time and energy to their borderland

Discourse, only to return more seriously to school in the third year. Once again, for Wilma there is more at school than the school's Discourses.

If we look at her eighth- and ninth-grade stories, we can see that conflict between her group's social practices and the school's, as well as her group's control over their own experience, is an issue that runs throughout the text as a whole. As we have just seen, in the eighth grade her growing mastery of the school leads to her "not bothering" with the school's rules. She has a enjoyed this year greatly ("had a nice time and enjoy every bit of it"), expressing a value that is certainly not part of school-based Discourses.

In the ninth grade she accepts, on her own terms, the school's rules, but also shows she understands ways of manipulating them (you deal with the teacher differently in front of the class than you do one-on-one). She concludes with "But don't let her take over you at all," a plea not to cede control to the teacher and the school even while living within the confines of that system.

Wilma enacts in thought, word, and values her own adolescent-based, community-based secondary Discourse, which is at various points in conflict with the school, but which has as one of its reasons for existing the function of mediating her own and her peers' interactions with the dominant, but often hostile "public sphere" Discourses of the school.

It is often said (see, for example, Willis, 1977) that the values embedded in a Discourse like Wilma's play a role in replicating her parent's place toward the bottom of the social hierarchy, since her resistance to the school will lead to a lack of school success and thus a poor economic future (see also Hebdige, 1979). While there is undoubtedly some truth in this, it misses the fact that an adolescent like Wilma knows that the school is unlikely to accept and value her community's social practices and give that community, on a full and fair basis, access to dominant secondary Discourses and the "goods" that go with them. Her borderland Discourse is a form of self-defense against colonization, which like all organized resistance to power is not always successful but does not always fail. Her text displays full mastery of and control over this secondary Discourse, and as such it is a prototypical instance of literacy.

But now we cannot fail to note that it will be a difficult matter indeed for Wilma to attain a full and meaningful apprenticeship within the school's Discourses, first because schools (and the wider Discourses of the elite and powerful whose interest our schools best represent) do not often offer such full and meaningful apprenticeships to minority and lower socioeconomic children but, also, because Wilma's borderland

Discourse is defined in part in opposition to the school's Discourses. In becoming a full member of school-based Discourses, she would be defining herself in opposition to herself.

This does not render the situation hopeless. Wilma's situation is more or less the plight of all of us, and certainly those of us who belong to, or were raised in, Discourses outside the "mainstream" of power and status in the wider society. None of us are completely consistent, unitary identities. We all play many roles, take on many different, sometimes conflicting identities within different Discourses. And sometimes we *do* change the dominant Discourses we achieve mastery over and, thus too, the society at large.

As we argued in the last chapter, "maladaptation" to Discourses, including the dominant Discourses of our society, can lead to "metaknowledge" and insight. It is precisely because a girl like Wilma, given her experiences within her communities and within the wider society, has such capacity to change the Discourses of power in our society that elites oppose her real entry into these Discourses or encourage her to disown her own primary and community Discourses should she actually gain such entrance. But though they often succeed in this, they do not always do so. Indeed, it is the few Wilmas who gain entry into Discourses of power without disowning their other Discourses who are the true seeds of change and salvation in American society—if, indeed, any such change is possible apart from revolutionary disruptions in our social structure (caused by economic, demographic, ecological, political, or social upheavals).

I hope it is clear through my discussion of Wilma, as well as the discussion throughout this book, that to study Wilma's writing, speaking, believing, valuing, memories, or meaning is not primarily to study what is going on inside Wilma's head. It is to study what is going on in the material and social world around Wilma within her specific Discourses. Wilma's mind, like each of ours, lies about out in the material, political, and social world. To retreat from this world is to retreat both from any viable linguistics or psychology, and from any hope of changing the world we live in.

I argued in Chapter 4 that the human mind, both in evolutionary terms and in its neurobiological structure, is expert at self-deception. This self-deception has led us to a world of violence, pollution, and injustice. If we humans are to survive with anything like justice and dignity, we need to *practice* more humane and life-enhancing meanings and memories in our social worlds. And this is something we must *do* together out in the world; it is not something that can be done privately inside our heads. That is *not* where the action is.

REFERENCES

Abrams, M. H. (1953). *The Mirror and the lamp: Romantic theory and the critical tradition*. Oxford: Oxford University Press.

Adams, M. J. (1990). *Beginning to read: Thinking and learning about print*. Cambridge, Mass.: MIT Press.

Alexander, R. D. (1971). The search for an evolutionary philosophy of man. *Proceedings of the Royal Society of Victoria* 84:99-120.

_____. (1989). The evolution of the human psyche. In P. Mellars & C. Stringer, eds., *The human revolution*. Princeton, N. J.: Princeton University Press.

Allman, W. F. (1989). *Apprentices of wonder: Inside the neural network revolution*. New York: Bantam.

Alverson, H., & Rosenberg, S. (1990). Discourse analysis of schizophrenic speech: A critique and proposal. *Applied Psycholinguistics* 11:167-84.

Atran, S. (1990). *Cognitive foundations of natural history: Towards an anthropology of science*. Cambridge: Cambridge University Press.

Bakhtin, M. M. (1981). *The dialogic imagination* (edited by M. Holquist. Austin: University of Texas Press.

_____. (1986). *Speech genres and other essays* (translated by V. W. McGee and edited by C. Emerson & M. Holquist). Austin: University of Texas.

Barthes, R. (1968). *Elements of semiology* (translated by Annette Lavers and Colin Smith. New York: Hill & Wang.

_____. (1975). *The pleasure of the text* (translated by Richard Miller). New York: Hill & Wang.

Bartlett, E. C. (1932). *Remembering: A study in experimental and social psychology*. New York: Macmillan; Cambridge: Cambridge University Press.

Belenky, M. F., Clinchy, B. M., Goldberger, N. R., & Tarule, J. M. (1986). *Women's ways of knowing: The development of self, voice, and mind.* New York: Basic Books.

Belsey, C. (1980). *Critical practice.* London: Methuen.

Bettelheim, B. (1982). Freud and the soul. *New Yorker,* March 1, pp. 52–93.

Bickerton, D. (1990). *Language and species.* Chicago: University of Chicago Press.

Binford, L. R. (1981). *Bones: Ancient men and modern myths.* New York: Academic Press.

_____. (1983). *In pursuit of the past.* London: Thames & Hudson.

_____. (1987). The hunting hypothesis, archeological methods and the past. *Yearbook of Physical Anthropology* 30:11–20.

Birch, D. (1989). *Language, literature and critical practice: Ways of analyzing text.* London: Routledge.

Bissex, G. L. (1980). *GNYS AT WRK: A child learns to write and read.* Cambridge, Mass.: Harvard University Press.

Bleich, D. (1978). *Subjective criticism.* Baltimore: Johns Hopkins University Press.

Bobrow, D. G., & Collins, A., eds. (1975). *Representation and understanding.* New York: Academic Press.

Bourdieu, P. (1977). *Outline of a theory of practice* (translated by R. Nice). Cambridge: Cambridge University Press.

_____. (1984). *Distinction: A social critique of the judgment of taste* (trans. by R. Nice). Cambridge, Mass.: Harvard University Press.

_____. (1990). *In other words: Essays towards a reflexive sociology.* Stanford, Calif.: Stanford University Press.

Bourdieu, P., & Passeron, J. C. (1977). *Reproduction in education, society and culture* (translated by R. Nice). London: Sage.

Bruner, J. (1977). Early social interaction and language development. In H. R. Schaffer, ed., *Studies in mother-child interaction.* London: Academic Press.

_____. (1983). *Child's talk: Learning to use language.* Oxford: Oxford University Press.

Byrne, R., & Whiten, A. (1987). The thinking primate's guide to deception. *New Scientist,* December 3, pp. 54–57.

_____. eds. (1988). *Machiavellian intelligence.* Oxford: Oxford University Press.

Callinicos, A. (1988). *Making history: Agency, structure and change in social theory.* Ithaca, N.Y.: Cornell University Press.

Campbell, J. (1990). *Transformations of myth through time.* New York: Harper & Row.

Cazden, C. (1988). *Classroom discourse: The language of teaching and learning.* Portsmouth, N.H: Heinemann.

Chall, J. (1967). *Learning to read: The great debate.* New York: McGraw-Hill.

Chall, J., Jacobs, V. A., and Baldwin, L. E. (1990). *The reading crisis: Why poor children fall behind*. Cambridge, Mass.: Harvard University Press.

Chomsky, N. (1975). *Reflections on language*. New York: Pantheon Books.

———. (1986). *Knowledge of language: Its nature, origin, and use*. New York: Praeger.

———. (1988). *Language and problems of knowledge: The Managua lectures*. Cambridge, Mass.: MIT Press.

Churchland, P. M. (1989). *A neurocomputational perspective: The nature of mind and the structure of science*. Cambridge, Mass.: MIT Press.

Churchland, P. S. (1986). *Neurophilosophy: Toward a unified science of the mind/brain*. Cambridge, Mass.: MIT Press.

Cialdini, R. B. (1984). *Influence: The new psychology of persuasion*. New York: Quill.

Clanchy, M. T. (1979). *From memory to written record: England; 1066–1307*. London: Edward Arnold.

Clark, A. (1989). *Microcognition: Philosophy, cognitive science, and parallel distributed processing*. Cambridge, Mass.: MIT Press.

Clay, M. M. (1976). *Young fluent readers*. London: Heinemann.

Clifford, J. (1988). *The predicament of culture: Twentieth-century ethnography, literature, and art*. Cambridge, Mass.: Harvard University Press.

Connerton, P. (1989). *How societies remember*. Cambridge: Cambridge University Press.

Cook-Gumperz, J., Ed. (1986). *The social construction of literacy*. Cambridge: Cambridge University Press.

Cresswell, M. J. (1990). Review of Bach: Informal lectures on formal semantics, *Language* 66:392–96.

Culler, J. (1982). *On deconstruction: Theory and criticism after structuralism*. Ithaca, N.Y.: Cornell University Press.

D'Andrade, R. (1987). A folk model of the mind. In *Cultural models in language and thought*, pp.112–48. *See* Holland and Quinn, eds., 1987.

Davis, G. (1985). *I got the Word in me and I can sing it, you know: A study of the performed African sermon*. Philadelphia: University of Pennsylvania Press.

Dawkins, R. (1976). *The selfish gene*. Oxford: Oxford University Press.

———. (1987). *The blind watchmaker: Why the evidence of evolution reveals a university without design*. New York: Norton.

Delpit, L. D. (1986). Skills and other dilemmas of a progressive educator. *Harvard Educational Review* 56:379–85.

———. (1988). The silenced dialogue: Power and pedagogy in educating other people's children. *Harvard Educational Review* 58:280–98.

Dennett, D. C. (1984). *Brainstorms: Philosophical essays on mind and psychology*. Cambridge, Mass.: MIT Press.

Derrida, J. (1976). *Of grammatology* (translated by Gayatri Chakravorty Spivak). Baltimore: Johns Hopkins University Press.

Desmond, A. (1989). *The politics of evolution: Morphology, medicine, and reform in radical London.* Chicago: University of Chicago Press.

Douglas, M. (1986). *How institutions think.* Syracuse, N.Y.: Syracuse University Press.

Eagleton, T. (1983). *Literary theory: An introduction.* Minneapolis: University of Minnesota Press.

————. (1984). *The functions of criticism: From the spectator to poststructuralism.* London: Verso.

————. (1990). *The ideology of the aesthetic.* Oxford: Basil Blackwell.

Edelman, M. (1988). *Constructing the political spectacle.* Chicago: University of Chicago Press.

Erickson, F. (1987). Transformation and school success: The politics and culture of educational achievement. *Anthropology and Education Quarterly* 18:335–56.

Erlich, P. R. (1986). *The machinery of nature: The living world around us—and how it works.* New York: Simon and Schuster.

Fairclough, N. (1989). *Language and power.* London: Longman.

Fausto-Sterling, A. (1985). *Myths of gender: Biological theories about women and men.* New York: Basic Books.

Feyerabend, P. K. (1981). *Philosophical papers.* 2 vols. Cambridge: Cambridge University Press.

Fillmore, C. (1975). An alternative to checklist theories of meaning. In *Proceedings of the First Annual Meeting of the Berkeley Linguistics Society*, pp. 123–131. Berkeley: University of California.

Finnegan, R. (1988). Speech, language and non-literacy: The Limba of Sierra Leone. In Ruth Finnegan, *Literacy and orality*, pp. 45–58. Oxford: Basil Blackwell.

Fish, S. (1980). *Is there a text in this class? The authority of interpretive communities.* Cambridge, Mass.: Harvard University Press.

Fleck, L. (1979). *The genesis and development of a scientific fact.* Chicago: University of Chicago Press.

Fodor, J. A. (1983). *Modularity of mind.* Cambridge, Mass.: MIT Press.

Foss, D. J. & Hakes, D. T. (1978). *Psycholinguistics: An introduction to the psychology of language.* Englewood Cliffs, N.J.: Prentice-Hall.

Foucault, M. (1972). *The archeology of knowledge* (translated by A. M. Sheridan Smith). New York: Harper & Row.

————. (1973). *The birth of the clinic: An archaeology of medical perception* (translated by Alan Sheridan). New York: Vintage Books.

————. (1977). *Discipline and punish: The birth of the prison* (translated by Alan Sheridan). New York: Pantheon.

————. (1978). *The History of sexuality*, Vol. 1: *An introduction* (translated by Robert Hurley). New York: Pantheon.

———. (1980). *Power/knowledge: Selected interviews and other writings, 1972-1977* (edited by C. Gordon, L. Marshall, J. Meplam, & K. Soper). Brighton, Sussex: Harvester Press.

———. (1985). *The Foucault reader* (edited by Paul Rainbow). New York: Pantheon.

Freccero, J. (1986). Autobiography and narrative, in T. C. Heller, M. Sosna, & D. E. Wellbery, eds., *Reconstructing individualism: Autonomy, individuality, and the self in Western thought*, pp. 16-29. Stanford, Calif.: Stanford University Press.

Frege, G. (1892). Uber Sinn and Bedeutung. *Zeitschrift für Philosophie und philosophische Kritik*, pp. 22-50. (English translation in P. Geach & M. Black, eds., *Translations from the philosophical writings of Gottlob Frege.* Oxford: Oxford University Press, 1980).

Gardner, H. (1983). *Frames of mind: The theory of multiple intelligences.* New York: Basic Books.

———. (1985). *The mind's new science: A history of the cognitive revolution.* New York: Basic Books.

Garfield, J. L., ed. (1987). *Modularity in knowledge representation and natural-language understanding.* Cambridge, Mass.: MIT Press.

Garnham, A. (1985). *Psycholinguistics: Central topics.* London: Methuen.

Gazzaniga, M. S. (1983). Right hemisphere language following brain bisection: A twentieth year perspective. *American Psychologist* 38:525-37.

———. (1985). *The social brain: Discovering the networks of the mind.* New York: Basic Books.

———. (1988). *Mind matters: How mind and brain interact to create our conscious lives.* Boston: Houghton Mifflin.

Gazzaniga, M. S., & Le Doux, J. E. (1978). *The integrated mind.* New York: Plenum.

Gee, J. P. (1986). Units in the production of narrative discourse. *Discourse Processes* 9:391-422.

———. (1987). What is literacy? *Teaching and Learning* 2:3-11.

———. (1988a). Discourse systems and aspirin bottles: On literacy. *Journal of Education* 170:27-40.

———. (1988b). Count Dracula, The Vampire Lestat, and TESOL. *TESOL Quarterly* 22:201-25.

———. (1989a). *Literacy, discourse, and linguistics: Essays by James Paul Gee.* Special issue of the *Journal of Education*, 171, edited by Candace Mitchell.

———. (1989b). What do English teacher's teach? In Gee, 1989a, pp. 135-46.

———. (1989c). Two styles of narrative construction and their linguistic and educational implications. *Discourse Processes* 12:287-307.

———. (1990a). A linguistic approach to narrative. *Journal of Narrative and Life History*, 1:15-93.

——. (1990b). Memory and myth: A perspective on narrative. In Allyssa McCabe & Carole Peterson, Eds., *Developing Narrative Structure*, pp. 1–25. Hillsdale, N.J.: Lawrence Erlbaum.

——. (1990c). *Social linguistics and literacies: Ideology in Discourses*. London: Falmer Press.

——. (1992). *Fundamental concepts in linguistics: An introduction to human language*. Englewood Cliffs, N. J.: Prentice-Hall.

Gee, J. P., Michaels, S., & O'Connor, C. (1991). Discourse analysis. In Margaret D. LeCompte, Judith P. Goetz, & Wendy Millroy, eds, *Handbook of Qualitative Research*. New York: Academic Press.

Geertz, C. (1973). *The interpretation of culture*. New York: Basic Books.

Giddens, A. (1984). *The constitution of society*. Berkeley: University of California Press.

——. (1990). *The consequences of modernity*. Stanford, Calif.: Stanford University Press.

Gilbert, D., and Kahl, J.A. (1987). *The American class structure: A new synthesis*. 3d ed. Chicago: Dorsey Press.

Gilligan, C. (1982). *In a different voice*. Cambridge, Mass.: Harvard University Press.

——. (1986). Remapping the moral domain: New images of the self in relationship. In T. C. Heller, M. Sosna, & D. E. Wellbery, eds. *Reconstructing individualism: Autonomy, individuality, and the self in Western thought*, pp. 237–52. Stanford, Calif.: Stanford University Press.

Givon, T. (1979). *On understanding grammar*. New York: Academic Press.

——. (1989). *Mind code and context: Essays in pragmatics*. Hillsdale, N.J.: Lawrence Erlbaum.

Goldschmidt, W. (1990). *The human career: The self in the symbolic world*. Oxford: Basil Blackwell.

Goodall, J. (1986). *The chimpanzees of Gombe: Patterns of behavior*. Cambridge, Mass.: Harvard University Press.

Goody, J. (1977). *The domestication of the savage mind*. Cambridge: Cambridge University Press.

——. (1986). *The logic of writing and the organization of society*. Cambridge: Cambridge University Press.

Gorman, R. P., & Sejnowski, T. J. (1988a). Learned classification of sonar targets using a massively parallel network, *IEEE Transactions: Acoustics, Speech, and Signal Processing*.

——. (1988b). Analysis of hidden units in a layered network trained to classify sonar targets. *Neural Networks* 1:75–89.

Graff, G. (1987). *Professing literature: An institutional history*. Chicago: University of Chicago Press.

Graff, H. J. (1987). *The legacies of literacy: Continuities and contradictions in western culture and society*. Bloomington: Indiana University Press.

Greene, G., & Kahn, C., Eds. (1985). *Making a difference: Feminist literary criticism*. London: Methuen.

Hacking, I. (1986). Making up people. In T. C. Heller, M. Sosna, & D. E. Wellbery, eds., *Reconstructing individualism: Autonomy, individuality, and the self in Western thought*, pp. 222–36, Stanford, Calif.: Stanford University Press.

Hanson, R. N. (1958). *Patterns of discovery*. Cambridge: Cambridge University Press.

Heath, S. B. (1983). *Ways with words: Language, life, and work in communities and classrooms*. Cambridge: Cambridge University Press.

Hebb, D. O. (1949). *The organization of behavior*. New York: Wiley.

Hebdige, D. (1979). *Subculture: The meaning of style*. London: Methuen.

Hewitt, R. (1986). *White talk black talk: Inter-racial friendship and communication amongst adolescents*. Cambridge: Cambridge University Press.

Hirsch, E. D., Jr. (1987). *Cultural literacy: What every American needs to know*. Boston: Houghton Mifflin, 1987.

Hodge, R. (1990). *Literature as discourse: Textual strategies in English and history*. Baltimore: Johns Hopkins University Press.

Hodge, R. & Kress, G. (1988). *Social semiotics*. Ithaca, N.Y.: Cornell University Press.

Holland, D., & Quinn, N, eds. (1987). *Cultural models in language and thought*. Cambridge: Cambridge University Press.

Holland, D., & Skinner, D. (1987). Prestige and intimacy. In *Cultural models in language and thought*, pp. 78–111. *See* Holland and Quinn, eds., 1987.

Holton, G. (1988). *Thematic origins of scientific thought: Kepler to Einstein*. Rev. ed. Cambridge, Mass.: Harvard University Press.

Hopper, P., & Thompson, S. (1980). Transitivity in grammar and discourse, *Language* 56:251–99.

———. .eds. (1982). *Syntax and semantics 15: Studies in transitivity*. New York: Academic Press.

Jackendoff, R. (1983). *Semantics and cognition*. Cambridge, Mass.: MIT Press.

———. (1987). *Consciousness and the computational mind*. Cambridge, Mass.: MIT Press.

———. (1990). *Semantic structures*. Cambridge, Mass.: MIT Press.

Jackson, P. (1989). *Maps of meaning: An introduction to cultural geography*. London: Unwin.

Jameson, F. (1981). *The political unconscious: Narrative as a socially symbolic act*. London: Methuen.

Johanson, D., & Shreeve, J. (1989). *Lucy's child: The discovery of a human ancestor*. New York: Avon Books.

Johnson, G. (1991). *In the palaces of memory: How we build the worlds inside our heads*. New York: Alfred A. Knopf.

Johnson, P. (1976). *A history of Christianity*. New York: Atheneum.

Johnson, R. C., & Brown, C. (1988). *Cognizers: Neural networks and machines that think.* New York: John Wiley.

Johnson-Laird, P. N. (1983). *Mental models: Towards a cognitive science of language, inference, and consciousness.* Cambridge, Mass.: Harvard University.

————. (1988). *The computer and the mind: An introduction to cognitive science.* Cambridge, Mass.: Harvard University Press.

Krashen, S. (1985a). *Inquiries and insights.* Hayward, Calif.: Alemany Press.

————. (1985b). *The Input Hypothesis: Issues and implications.* London: Longman.

Kuhn, T. S. (1970). *The structure of scientific revolutions.* (2d. ed. Chicago: University of Chicago Press.

Labov, W. (1972a). *Sociolinguistic patterns.* Philadelphia: University of Pennsylvania Press.

————. (1972b). *Language in the inner city.* Philadelphia: University of Pennsylvania Press.

————. (1972c). The transformation of experience in narrative syntax. In W. Labov, *Language in the inner city,* pp. 354–96. Philadelphia, Pa.: University of Pennsylvania Press.

Labov, W., & Fanshel, D. (1977). *Therapeutic discourse: Psychotherapy as conversation.* New York: Academic Press.

Labov, W., & Waletsky, J. (1967). Narrative analysis: Oral versions of personal experience. In J. Helm, ed., *Essays on the verbal and visual arts.* Seattle: University of Washington Press.

Lakoff, G. (1986). *Women, fire, and other dangerous things.* Chicago: University of Chicago Press.

Lakoff, G., & Johnson, M. (1980). *Metaphors we live by.* Chicago: University of Chicago Press.

Langer, E. J. (1989). *Mindfulness.* Cambridge, Mass.: Harvard University Press.

Laqueur, T. (1990). *Making sex: Body and gender from the Greeks to Freud.* Cambridge, Mass.: Harvard University Press.

Lave, J. (1988). *Cognition in practice.* Cambridge: Cambridge University Press.

Leach, E., (1969). *"Genesis as myth" and other essays.* London: Jonathan Cape.

————. (1976). *Culture and communication: The logic by which symbols are connected.* Cambridge: Cambridge University Press.

Leach, E., & Aycock, D.A. (1983). *Structuralist interpretations of biblical myth.* Cambridge: Cambridge University Press.

Levelt, W.J.M. (1989). *Production: From intention to articulation.* Cambridge, Mass.: MIT Press.

Levinson, S. (1983). *Pragmatics.* Cambridge University Press.

Levi-Strauss, C. (1963). *Structural anthropology.* New York: Basic Books.

————. (1964–1971). *Mythologiques.* 4 volumes. Paris: Plon.

_____. (1966). *The Savage Mind.* Chicago: University of Chicago Press.

_____. (1979). *Myth and Meaning.* New York: Schocken Books.

Lorne, E. (1943). *Cézanne's Composition.* Berkeley: University of California Press.

Luke, A. (1988). *Literacy, textbooks and ideology.* London: Falmer.

MacArthur, R. H. (1972). *Geographical ecology.* New York: Harper & Row.

McClelland, J., Rumelhart, D., & Hinton, G. (1986). The appeal of PDP. In *Parallel distributed processing: Explorations in the microstructure of cognition,* Vol. 1, pp. 3–44. *See* D. Rumelhart, J. McClelland, & the PDP Research Group, 1986.

McClelland, J., Rumelhart, D., & the PDP Research Group (1986). *Parallel distributed processing: Explorations in the microstructure of cognition,* Vol. 2. Cambridge, Mass.: MIT Press.

McDermott, R. (1987a). Achieving school failure: An anthropological approach to illiteracy and social stratification, in G. Spindler, Ed., *Education and cultural process: Anthropological approaches,* 2nd ed., pp. 173–209. Prospects Heights, IL: Waveland Press.

_____. (1987b). The explanation of minority failure, again, *Anthropology and Education Quarterly* 18:361–364.

Macdonell, D. (1986). *Theories of discourse: An introduction.* Oxford: Basil Blackwell.

Mack, N. (1989). The social nature of words: Voices, dialogues, quarrels, *The Writing Instructor* 8:157–65.

McLaughlin, B. (1987). *Theories of second-language learning.* London: Edward Arnold.

Mandler, J. M. (1984). *Stories, scripts, and scenes: Aspects of schema theory.* Hillsdale, N.J.: Erlbaum.

Manktelow, K. I., & Over, D. E. (1990). *Inference and understanding: A philosophical and psychological perspective.* London: Routledge.

Michaels, S. (1981). Sharing time: Children's narrative styles and differential access to literacy. *Language in Society,* 10: 423–42.

_____. (1990). Literacy as reasoning within multiple discourses: Implications for policy and educational reform. Paper presented to the Council of Chief State School Officers Summer Institute on Restructuring Learning.

Michaels, S., & Collins, J. (1984). Oral discourse styles: Classroom interaction and the acquisition of literacy. In D. Tannen, Ed., *Coherence in spoken and written discourse,* pp. 219–44. Norwood, N.J.: Ablex.

Middleton, D., & Edwards, E., eds. (1990). *Collective remembering.* London: Sage.

Miller, G. A., & Johnson-Laird, P. N. (1976). *Language and perception.* Cambridge, Mass.: Harvard University Press.

Milroy, J., & Milroy, L. (1985). *Authority in language: Investigating language prescription and standardisation.* London: Routledge & Kegan Paul.

Moi, T. (1985). *Sexual textual politics.* London: Methuen.

Neisser, U. (1982). *Memory observed*. Oxford: Oxford University Press.

Neisser, U. & Winograd, E. (1988). *Remembering reconsidered: Ecological and traditional approaches to the study of memory*. Cambridge: Cambridge University Press.

Newman, D., Griffin, P., & Cole, M. (1989). *The construction zone: Working for cognitive change in school*. Cambridge: Cambridge University Press.

Nichols, P. C. (1989). Storytelling in Carolina: Continuities and contrasts. *Anthropology and Education Quarterly* 20:232–45.

Nisbett, R., & Ross, L. (1980). *Human inference: Strategies and shortcomings of social judgment*. Englewood Cliffs, N.J.: Prentice-Hall.

Norman, D. A. (1969). *Memory and attention: An introduction to human information processing*. New York: Wiley.

———. (1986). Reflections on cognition and parallel distributed processing. In *Parallel distributed processing: Explorations in the microstructure of cognition*, Vol. 2, pp. 110–46. *See* J. McClelland, D. Rumelhart, & the PDP Research Group, 1986.

———. (1988). *The psychology of eveyday things*. New York: Basic Books.

Ogbu, J. (1978). *Minority education and caste: The American system in cross-cultural perspective*. New York: Academic Press.

———. (1983). Minority status and schooling in plural societies. *Comparative Education Review* 27:168–90.

———. (1987). Variability in minority responses to schooling: Nonimmigrants vs. immigrants. In G. Spindler & L. Spindler, eds., *Interpretive ethnography of education: At home and abroad*, pp. 255–78. Hillsdale, N.J.: Lawrence Erlbaum.

Ong, W. J. (1958). *Ramus: Method and the decay of dialogue*. Cambridge, Mass.: Harvard University Press.

Ortony, A., Clore, G. L., & Collins, A. (1988). *The cognitive structure of emotions*. Cambridge University Press.

Peirce, C. S. (1940). *The philosophy of Peirce* (edited by J. Buchler). New York: Harcourt, Brace.

Pinker, S. (1989). *Learnability and cognition: The acquisition of argument structure*. Cambridge, Mass.: MIT Press.

Propp, V. (1968). *Morphology of the Russian folktale*. Austin: University of Texas Press. (Orginally published 1928.)

Putnam, H. (1975). The meaning of "meaning." In H. Putnam, *Mind, language, and reality*, pp. 215–71. Cambridge: Cambridge University Press.

Quigley, S. P. & Paul, P. V. (1984). *Language and deafness*. San Diego, Calif.: College-Hill Press.

Quinn, N., & Holland, D. (1987). Culture and cognition. In *Cultural models in language and thought*, pp. 3–40. *See* Holland and Quinn, eds., 1987.

Radford, A. (1990). *Syntactic theory and the acquisition of English syntax*. Oxford: Basil Blackwell.

Ricoeur, P. (1981). *Hermeneutics and the human sciences* (edited and translated by John B. Thompson). Cambridge: Cambridge University Press.

Rogoff, B., (1990). Apprenticeship in thinking: Cognitive development in social context. New York: Oxford University Press.

Rogoff, B., & Lave, J., eds. (1984). *Everyday cognition: Its development in social context.* Cambridge, Mass.: Harvard University Press.

Rosaldo, R. (1989). *Culture and truth: The remaking of social analysis.* Boston: Beacon Press.

Rose, M. (1989). *Lives on the boundary.* New York: Penguin.

Rumelhart, D., McClelland, J., & the PDP Research Group. (1986). *Parallel distributed processing: Explorations in the microstructure of cognition,* Vol. 1. Cambridge, Mass.: MIT Press.

Said, E. (1983). *The world, the text, and the critic.* Cambridge, Mass.: Harvard University Press.

Saussure, F. de. (1916). *Cours de linguistique generale.* Paris: Payot. (English translation. by Wade Baskin published as *A course in general linguistics.* New York: McGraw-Hill, 1959.)

Schank, R., & Abelson, R. (1977). *Scripts, plans, goals, and understanding.* Hillsdale, N.J.: Lawrence Erlbaum.

Schickedanz, J. A. (1986). *More than ABCs: The early stages of reading and writing.* Washington, D.C.: National Association for the Education of Young Children.

Schwartz, B. (1990). The reconstruction of Abraham Lincoln. In D. Middleton & D. Edwards, eds. *Collective Remembering,* pp. 81–107. London: Sage.

Scollon, R., & Scollon, S.B.K. (1981). *Narrative, literacy, and face in interethnic communication.* Norwood, N.J.: Ablex.

Scribner, S., & Cole, M. (1981). *The psychology of literacy.* Cambridge, Mass.: Harvard University Press.

Shotter, J. (1990). The social construction of remembering and forgetting. In D. Middleton & D. Edwards, eds., *Collective remembering,* pp. 120–38. London: Sage.

Shuman, A. (1986). *Storytelling rights: The uses of oral and written texts by urban adolescents.* Cambridge: Cambridge University Press.

Skehan, P. (1989). *Individual differences in second-language learning.* London: Edward Arnold.

Small, M. (1989). Social climber: Independent rise in rank by a female Barbary Macaque. Unpublished manuscript cited in Johanson & Shreeve, *Lucy's child,* pp. 273, 294.

Smitherman, G. (1977). *Talkin' and testifin': The language of black America.* Boston: Houghton Mifflin.

Snow, C. E. (1983). Literacy and language: Relationships in the preschool years. *Harvard Educational Review* 53:165–89.

———. (1986). Conversations with children. In P. Fletcher & M. Garman, *Language Acquisition*, 2nd ed., pp. 69–89. Cambridge: Cambridge University Press.

———. (1983). Literacy and language: Relationships in the preschool years. *Harvard Educational Review* 53:165–89.

Soja, E. W. (1988). *Postmodern geographies: The reassertion of space in social thought.* London: Verso.

Sternberg, R. J. (1990). *Metaphors of mind: Conceptions of the nature of intelligence.* Cambridge: Cambridge University Press.

Street, B. (1984). *Literacy in theory and practice.* Cambridge: Cambridge University Press.

Stuart, H., & Jefferson, T. (1976). *Resistance through rituals: Youth subcultures in post-war Britain.* London: Hutchinson, 1976.

Stuckey, S. (1987). *Slave culture: Nationalist theory and the foundations of black America.* New York: Oxford University Press.

Sutton, R. S., & Barto, A. G. (1981). Toward a modern theory of adpative networks: Expectation and prediction. *Psychological Review* 88:135–70.

Tannen, D. (1989). *Talking Voices: Repetition, Dialogue, and Imagery in Conversational Discourse.* Cambridge: Cambridge University Press.

Taylor, D. (1983). *Family literacy: Young children learning to read and write.* Portsmouth, N.H.: Heinemann.

Taylor, D., & Dorsey-Gaines, C. (1987). *Growing up literate: Learning from inner city families.* Portsmouth, N.H.: Heinemann.

Teale, W. H. (1986). Home background and young children's literacy development. In W. H. Teale & E. Sulzby, eds. *Emergent literacy*, pp. 173–206. Norwood, N.J.: Ablex.

Teale, W. H. & Sulzby, E., eds. (1986). *Emergent literacy.* Norwood, N.J.: Ablex.

Tharp, R., and Gallimore, R. (1988). *Rousing minds to life: Teaching, learning, and schooling in social context.* Cambridge: Cambridge University Press.

Thompson, J. B. (1984). *Studies in the theory of ideology.* Berkeley: University of California Press.

Todd, J. (1988). *Feminist literary history.* New York: Routledge.

Toffler, A. (1990). *Powershift: Knowledge, wealth, and violence at the edge of the 21st century.* New York: Bantam.

Toril, M. (1985). *Sexual textual politics.* London: Methuen.

Trueba, H. T., ed. (1987). *Success or failure?: Learning and the language minority student.* New York: Newbury House.

———. (1989). *Raising silent voices: Educating linguistic minorities for the twenty-first century.* Cambridge, Mass.: Newbury House.

Voloshinov, V. (1973). *Marxism and the philosophy of language* (translated by L. Matejks & I. R. Titunik). New York: Seminar Press. (Original ed. 1929.)

Vygotsky, L. S. (1987). *The collected works of L. S. Vygotsky,* Vol. 1: *Problems of general psychology. Including the volume Thinking and speech.* (edited by R. W. Rieber & A. S. Carton). New York: Plenum.

Wells, G. (1981). *Learning through interaction.* Cambridge: Cambridge University Press.

_____. (1985). *Language development in the pre-school years.* Cambridge: Cambridge University Press.

_____. (1986). *The meaning makers: Children learning language and using language to learn.* Portsmouth, N.H.: Heinemann.

White, H. (1973). *Metahistory: The historical imagination in Nineteenth-Century Europe.* Baltimore: Johns Hopkins University Press.

_____. (1978). *Tropics of discourse: Essays in cultural criticism.* Baltimore: Johns Hopkins University Press.

Willinsky, J. (1990). *The new literacy: Redefining reading and writing in the schools.* New York: Routledge.

Willis, P. (1977). *Learning to labour.* London: Saxon House.

Wittgenstein, L. (1958). *Philosophical investigations* (Translated by G.E.M. Anscombe). New York: Macmillan.

Wolfram, W., & Fasold, R. W. (1964). *The study of social dialects in American English.* Englewood Cliffs, N.J.: Prentice-Hall.

INDEX

default values, filling in, 42–43
descriptions: concepts and, 25; images and, 24; partial, 41; schemas and, 42
developmental evaluation, 135
differences, knowledge of, 33
Discourses, 49; acquisition vs. learning, 113–19; apprenticeship and, 104, 114–15, 125; associative links and, 108; bird-watching and, 87–88; borderland, 146–51; carriers of, 132; conflicting, 109, 110, 111, 150; criticism of, 112; defined, 20; disciplining by, 88; education and, 119–24; folk theories and, 108; as gates to society, 117–18; ideological, 141–42; literacy and, 119–33; and literature, 112; mastered through acquisition, 114–15; new, emergent, 111; opposing, 112, 141; political, 141; primary, 108–12; props and, 108; school-based, 119–37; secondary, 108–12, 147, 150; social group membership and, 107; social institutions and, 108; social practices and, 91, 114–15; society and, 107–13; tools for, 90
discrimination, perceptual features and, 34–35
distributed parallel processing, 25
distributive justice, xix
domination, 101, 111

ecological dominance, 102
Edelman, Murray, 64
education, xix; Discourses and, 119–24; minorities and, 119–24. *See also* schools
emotional system, brain's modules and, 98

emotional turmoil, exploration of, 82
emplotting, 65, 89
encoding information, 38, 63. *See also* linguistic encoding
enculturation, 114
endings, markers for, 59
environmental pressure, intelligence and, 99–100
epilepsy, 93
epiphenomena, 65
episodes, 60, 63, 65
episodic memory, 61
episodic structuring, 63, 67, 77–78, 89
errors, inhibitory links and, 41
essayist Discourses, 145
essayist literacy, 19
events, background and foreground, 57–61
excitatory connection, 38, 43, 44
expectations, 59, 86–87, 91
experiences, 55; emplotting, 65, 89; episodically reporting, 89; learning and, 113, 115; linguistic encoding of, 57, 58–60; marginalizing, 7; mind modules and, 96–97; number in common, 48
experts, internal structure and, 7
explanations: brain's interpreter and, 97–98; split-brain patients and, 94–96

face recognition, 97
falsity, states of the world and, 4
features: clusters of, 39; network representation of, 45
Finnegan, Ruth, 116
folk theories, 21; apprenticeships and, 90; bird-watchers and, 84–88; brain's interpreter and, 98–105; corrected, 52; deviant, 108; Discourses and, 108; for-

About the Author

JAMES PAUL GEE, Professor of Linguistics at the University of Southern California, Los Angeles, is the recipient of many awards and major grants for his work in linguistics. He is the author of numerous articles and two previous books, the most recent of which is *Social Linguistics and Literacies*.